David,

Best wishes for a Happy Birthday
and many a birdie in the future!
With much love.
Robert, Suzanne + Mungo.

24 July '97

GOLF AT THE WATER'S EDGE

SCOTLAND'S SEASIDE LINKS

GOLF AT THE WATER'S EDGE

BRENDA AND JOHN McGUIRE

SCOTLAND'S SEASIDE LINKS

ABBEVILLE PRESS • PUBLISHERS ~ NEW YORK • LONDON • PARIS

Acknowledgments

We thank the greenkeepers, club secretaries, and golfers who welcomed us to their distinctive courses and clubhouses and shared insights about, and subtleties of, their courses.

Over the years our friends in Scotland have guided us to their favorite courses and told us of the ones they dream of playing. Thank you for many long dinner conversations.

We also thank Brian Hotchkiss and Peter Blaiwas of Vernon Press for their energy, which contributed to the publishing of this book.

Front cover: The clubhouse at St. Andrews
Back cover: The lighthouse near Turnberry Hotel Golf Club
Title-page: Elie — The Golf House Club

A Vernon Press Book
Production Manager: Lou Bilka

The text of this book was set in New Caledonia and Upper West Side typefaces.

Printed and bound in China

First edition
10 9 8 7 6 5 4 3 2 1

Library of Congress Cataloging-in-Publication Data
McGuire, Brenda.
    Golf at the water's edge : Scotland's seaside links / Brenda and John McGuire.
        p.   cm.
    Includes index.
    ISBN 0–7892–0323–5
    1. Golf courses—Scotland—Guidebooks.   I. McGuire, John M.,
    1949– . II. Title.
    GV975.M34 1997
    796.352'06'8411--dc21   96–39206

To our sons, Chris and Tim

CONTENTS

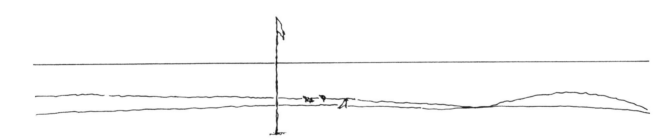

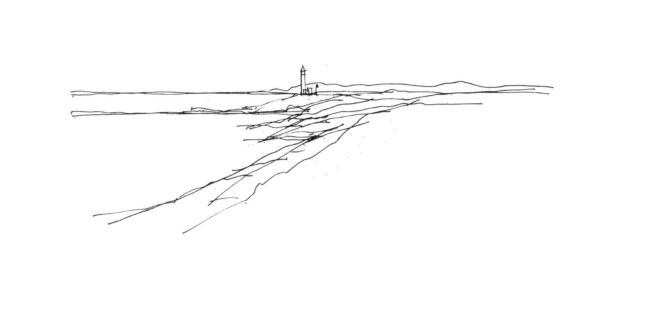

PREFACE

When I was growing up, the British Open Championship was the most important sporting event of the year in our family. My grandfather—who, had fate treated him differently, would have become a professional golfer—always brought the family together to watch on his small black-and-white television the greatest test of golf. This was an important event that was traditionally celebrated like a birthday, the Fourth of July, or Christmas. I participated in this annual ritual throughout my formative years. So, when I moved to Scotland with my own family, where we were to live for a time, I already knew the great links courses: Turnberry, Royal Troon, Royal Dornoch, Carnoustie, and, of course, St. Andrews. The links of the Old Course is the same stretch of sward where golf was played as long ago as the sixteenth century.

J.M.
Edinburgh
1995

INTRODUCTION

Elie—The Golf House Club

Bored shepherds near Rome are believed to have started batting about small rocks or nuts with the tops of their crooks. This idling pastime could have evolved into the popular game of *paganica,* from *paganus* or "country man," which was played by the Roman Legion during its occupation of Scotland in the first century B.C. Eventually this cross-country recreation was played with a bent stick and a leather ball stuffed with feathers. Some believe that the game of golf has its origins in this ancient Roman game.

A stronger case is to be made for Dutch influence in the origination of golf. Players of the early Dutch game of *kolven* (when played on ice) or *kolf* (when on the ground) used clubs with brass and wooden heads. The Low Dutch word *kolf* springs from the German noun *Kolbe,* or "club," so it follows that the game of golf is synonymous with the "game of club." When spoken, of course, *kolf* very closely resembles the English word *golf.* This theory of Dutch influence is strengthened by the fact that a game using clubs was depicted in more than four hundred Dutch paintings during the period from 1500 to 1700. The Dutch also would later become skilled makers of golf balls, which they then exported to Scotland.

Chole, a game played in the open countryside of Belgium and France, bore some resemblance to golf as well. In *chole,* each team of two players used one ball and played to a prearranged target, about one mile from the starting point. The target generally was a landmark, such as a gate, a church door, or the steps of a local inn.

In Britain the game of *cambuca* involved hitting a small ball made from boxroot. A stained-glass panel dating to about 1350, in the east window of Gloucester

Cathedral, shows a man clothed in a medieval robe just about to strike a ball with a club. In 1363 *cambuca*, along with other distracting games, was banned.

While the game's origin has long been discussed, there is little argument that most of golf's development occurred in Scotland. Playing a ball over the links is a Scottish game and no other. The first written record describing the sport dates from 1457, when James II of Scotland ruled that both "Fute-ball and Golfe be utterly cryed downe" because they interfered with the practice of archery, an important skill necessary for the defense of Scotland. Mary, Queen of Scots, was an avid golfer. She is credited with giving the term "caddie" to the person who carried her golf balls and clubs, and she was criticized for playing golf too soon after her second husband was murdered in 1567.

There is strong evidence a century later that James II's statutes had had little effect. In 1592, in an effort to protect Scottish piety, the town council of Edinburgh declared the "Sabboth Day" as the Lord's day and proclaimed that all citizens must dedicate themselves to the service of God. Golf was forbidden, in or out of town, and anyone caught so playing was subject to a fine. However, to stop the complaints of his people, James VI of Scotland—who loved the game and even had his own club maker—declared in 1618 that "after the end of divine service" his good people should not be disturbed, thus allowing golf to be played openly after church.

In 1682, James VII of Scotland played against two Englishmen at Holyrood Palace in the first international match. His partner was John Patersone, a local shoe-maker and the best shot maker in the kingdom. The Scottish team won and with his winnings Patersone built himself a fine house on the Royal Mile in Edinburgh.

When the Gentlemen Golfers of Leith set out their thirteen "Articles and

Bruntsfield Links

Laws in Playing at Golf," in 1744, the informality of the game ended. Nearly identical rules were adopted by the Society of St. Andrews Golfers on May 14, 1754, and these rules guided the development of golf.

Much of the game of golf became formalized in and around Edinburgh. One of the earliest golf courses, Bruntsfield Links, is near Edinburgh Castle on land similar to a seaside links course. The original six holes are now part of a short course on common land where golf is still played in front of the fifteenth-century Golf Tavern, which served as the meeting place for two of the oldest clubs in the world: the Royal Burgess Golfing Society (1735) and the Bruntsfield Golfing Society (1761).

Key to Map

East Lothian

1. North Berwick West Links
2. Winterfield Golf Club
3. Dunbar Golf Club
4. Longniddry Golf Club
5. Bruntsfield Links

West of Scotland

6. Western Gailes Golf Club
7. Royal Troon Golf Club
8. Prestwick Golf Club—Old Course
9. Prestwick St. Nicholas Golf Club
10. Belleisle Golf Course
11. Turnberry Hotel Golf Club

Fife

12. Elie—The Golf House Club
13. Crail—Balcomie Golf Course
14. St. Andrews—The Old Course

Northeast

15. Monifieth Golf Links
16. Panmure Golf Club
17. Carnoustie Golf Links
18. Montrose Links Trust

Highlands

19. Cruden Bay Golf Club
20. Nairn Golf Club
21. Royal Dornoch Golf Club

SCOTLAND

Inverness

Aberdeen

Glasgow

Edinburgh

THE SCOTTISH LINKS

St. Andrew's— The Old Course

Golf has been played over Scotland's seaside links for centuries. Links are the public lands held by the burgh for the common good of its citizens. Such linkslands provided a place where the citizens of the town or village could graze their animals, do their laundry, practice archery, and engage in a wide range of other activities, including sports. Of these, golf ultimately became the most popular.

These early courses were primarily left in a natural state and had no formal greens or tees. The fairways were watered when it rained, and were mowed by grazing sheep. There is no evidence of formal rules during these early days of golf for, in a sense, golf was more of a pastime than a sport—a pleasant diversion from the rigors of medieval life.

The village encouraged its citizens to play golf on this common land. These courses were practical, pleasurable, and built to suit everyone. The early courses that evolved on these links all followed similar principles, which promoted the use of the natural terrain as much as possible and eventually became the models for classic principles of golf-course design. For those who truly love the game, the windswept courses nestled in among the dunes and hillocks are the only places to play the ancient game of golf.

A remarkable range and variety of courses are to be found on the shores of Scotland. Their unique appeal lies in the exhilarating feeling of freedom and the expansive sense of space. For those who play on a modern course in a more sheltered setting among groves of trees and along placid lakes, Scottish courses provide a dramatic contrast. A golfer playing on a seaside links is exposed to the elements, some-

Crail—Balcomie Golf Course

times brutally. Playing over a natural links course in these demanding conditions requires rigor and discipline.

Over thousands of years of geological action, the seas along the shores of Scotland receded to leave a natural landscape ideally suited for the game of golf. Here have been created the classic links courses—some grand, some humble—that now occupy the unique linksland at the water's edge. Golf is a game that can be played in a wide variety of settings: over open heaths, in sheltered parks, on lonely moors, in dense woodlands, and on the ancient links by the sea where golf has its roots. Many believe that play on a traditional links is the only true form of the game. Today all of Britain's great golf championships are contested at seaside courses.

Links refers to the land between the sea and the more fertile ground, which is often no more than a couple hundred yards inland. This strip of land has no agricultural value, for only the fine, wiry grasses capable of growing in the sand can flourish here. Linksland provides an ideal surface for golf and is wonderful for iron play.

Course designers used the natural landscape as they found it. Because this landscape comprises only a thin ribbon of land along the sea, a links course is often only two holes wide. Greens are made in clearings, atop plateaus, or in dells, and are rarely level. The ultimate centerpiece of every hole, greens reveal the importance of correct angling, careful shaping, and discrete contouring. Tees are flat and often undefined. Bunkers are created in the hollows of the landscape and are strategically placed.

Fairways run between sandhills and gorse and are sometimes divided by burns or streams flowing to the sea. A traditional links fairway is a rolling ocean of humps and hollows that makes an even lie or stance rare. The rough along the fair-way is murderous, as Ben Hogan tells us:

> *Heather and gorse are abundant in the rough. Heather, something*
> *like a fern, grows in clumps about eight inches to a foot high and is*
> *thick as can be. If you get in it, you have to hit the ball about ten*
> *times as hard as you would otherwise and then most times it won't go*
> *more than ten yards or so. Gorse is taller, sometimes waist to head*
> *high and is a brambly bush. I don't know what you do if you get in it.*

It is difficult to tell where the fairway ends and the rough begins except when fair-ways run along the beach. Little is predictable about playing over a links course. There are no typical shots. Links golf requires players to use their imagination to overcome unexpected situations; improvisation is essential. Golfers must make the shots they can, not the ideal ones they would like to make.

The other test of the golfer's skill and nerve is the weather. Sun. Wind. Fog. Rain. One of these is always present during a match at a seaside course, and there are even occasions when all are present at the same time. All four seasons can be experi-enced in one day. The wind can change directions, sometimes minute by minute. The speed with which the weather changes along the sea is an important characteristic of a links course. Stranded at the far end of the course as the temperature drops, and rain, driven by a chilling wind, sweeps in from the sea, a golfer must show his skill and ability to play well in all situations. This is the way golf was intended to be played.

The finest way to understand the principles of golf is to play a seaside links.

Royal Dornoch Golf Club

Carnoustie Golf Links

Straight and accurate hitting is necessary to play in the undulating land between the dunes. The links illustrate the virtues of positional play and expose the dilemma of power play. Golfers who play over these courses must pay attention to even the smallest of details and understand the influence of both the land and the weather on the game. If you have played golf only on a modern parkland course, imagine how different—and rewarding—play must be on the ancient and legendary links courses at the water's edge in Scotland.

Hearing a man who has only recently discovered the game of golf holding forth on the beauty of what I should have thought to be a comparatively ordinary course, I fell to marvelling at the extraordinary variety of experience offered by this singular game and the extraordinary reluctance of the average player to take advantage of it.

Every other game is played on the same kind of pitch the world over. One football field is like another; one cricket pitch like the next, except that in one case the background may be the village chestnuts and in another the gasometers.

Yet not only is every golfing pitch different from all the others, but it consists of 18 little pitches within itself. Thus an almost inexhaustible supply of golfing problems presents itself.

—Henry Longhurst

Dunbar Golf Club

EAST LOTHIAN

East Lothian, just to the south and east of Edinburgh, offers a wider variety and larger number of courses within just a few miles of each other than any other place in the world. Given the requisite stamina, one could play a round of golf on two different courses every day of the week and still not have played all the courses in East Lothian.

This is the "Holy Land of Golf."

North Berwick
West Links

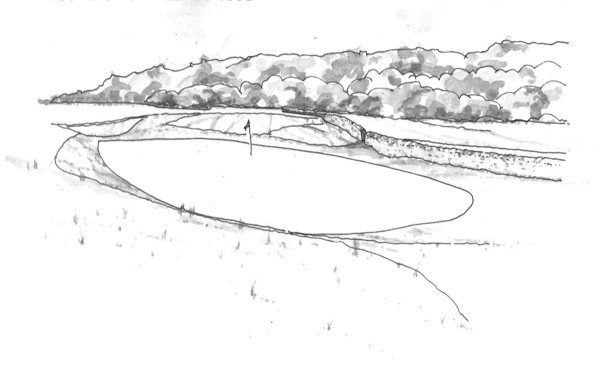

Founded in 1832, North Berwick Golf Club is one of the oldest and most distinguished clubs in the region. It has had a prime minister, Lord Balfour, as its captain (1891–92), and has been home to such important golfers as Ben Sayers, the famous club maker, and J. E. Laidley, winner of the Amateur Championship in St. Andrews in 1889 and 1891. The club awards the oldest trophy for junior golfers, the Elcho Medal (1867). Two famous and widely copied holes—Perfection and Redan, the 14th and the 15th, respectively—are found on this course.

North Berwick reflects ancient rather than modern golf, with blind shots, shots over Eil Burn, and shots over walls. This type of game can only be found at a seaside links. Wind and weather are part of golf and part of the challenge the golfer must be prepared to face, for it is possible to play the first nine holes in warm sunshine, then the last nine in a North Sea storm.

This great course begins near the center of town, wraps around the coast, then stretches out of sight along a narrow strip of land between beach and woods, where many fine houses look out over the course. All the holes are within sight of the Firth of Forth and are either behind a sand dune or next to the beach. The course itself is always ready to penalize the slightly overconfident golfer.

True to its name, the 14th hole, Perfection, requires just that. It is a 376-yard par 4 with a slight dogleg entry to the green. The first shot must miss a group of bunkers to the right. The second, over a big hill, needs to reach a hidden green set right next to the beach.

Redan, the other renowned hole, follows. This short 192-yard par 3 is one of the most difficult holes there is. The green is flanked to left and right by a series of deep, well-placed bunkers. Once golfers reach the plateau they find the green sloping away from them.

Those may be the most famous holes, but old-timers say that the fun really begins at the Pit (hole 13), a 365-yard par 4. This quaint hole has a short dogleg to the left over a stone wall that protects a sunken green. The course guide reminds the golfer to "drive right of centre and don't argue with the wall, it's older than you."

Splendid views across the Firth of Forth are available from just about everywhere on the course. The best-known landmark in the firth, Bass Rock, is home to thousands of seabirds and a thriving colony of seals. As golfers reach the 18th and head toward town, their view is dominated by Berwick Law, an impressive cone-shaped volcanic hill that rises quickly to a height of 663 feet. Just east of town the ruins of Tantallon Castle cling to the top of a cliff.

The course at North Berwick is open to all visitors.

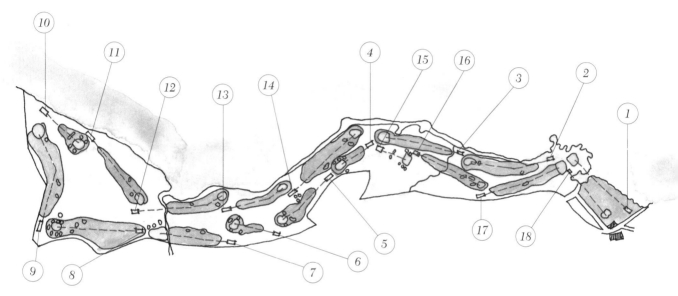

North

NORTH BERWICK
WEST LINKS

1. Point Garry (out)
2. Sea
3. Trap
4. Carlekemp
5. Bunkershill
6. Quarry
7. Eil Burn
8. Linkhouse
9. Mizzentop
10. Eastward Ho!
11. Bos'ns Locker
12. Bass
13. Pit
14. Perfection
15. Redan
16. Gate
17. Point Garry (in)
18. Home

Winterfield Golf Club

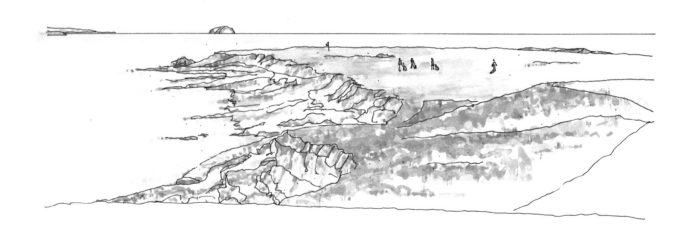

At the west end of the Burgh of Dunbar, Winterfield Golf Club sits on a series of terraces overlooking the Firth of Forth and Belhaven Bay. Originally, Winterfield Mains was a long-established farm owned by Sir Robert Usher. In 1886, Sir Robert gave his daughter Margaret a wedding gift of land on which she and her husband built their home between 1904 and 1906. St. Margaret's, an elegant red-sandstone house, remained in the family until 1939, when it was requisitioned by the War Department. During World War II, this stately house sheltered troops who manned the pillboxes along Belhaven Bay. In 1972, St. Margaret's became the clubhouse for the Winterfield Golf and Sports Club. Of all the clubhouses in East Lothian, St. Margaret's offers the most strikingly beautiful view of sea, sky, and course.

Winterfield Mains remained a farm until 1930, when the land was sold and a course laid out. The original course, which was very different from today's layout, was requisitioned along with St. Margaret's during World War II. Hundreds of antitank blocks were constructed and the course was fitted with dozens of searchlights, thus becoming part of Great Britain's coastal defense. The War Department underwrote restoration of the course in 1946, and the layout is now a mix of parkland holes and traditional links holes.

Only 5,155 yards long, Winterfield is a short course, with eight par 3s. However, it is constructed in such a manner that only the very best shots pay dividends. Numerous bunkers await any shot that is the least bit off line. The beach or cliffs along the firth are adjacent to the 1st, 13th, 14th, and 15th holes.

The opening hole, Whelkie Haugh, is no easy start. It requires an almost perfect shot across an enormous gully that stretches from tee to green. If golfers miss that tee shot to the green, they may find their very first shot in the firth. This opening becomes even less attractive when they realize that this is only the first par 3, with seven more to follow. The 7th hole, at 438 yards, is not particularly difficult, but since the North Road runs parallel to the fairway, the slightest hook will be out of bounds. Overlooking Belhaven Bay and Bass Rock, the 16th tee offers one of the finest views on any golf course.

The annual open competition is staged in July for the Craig-en-Gelt Trophy; in September the St. Margaret's Open is held.

Dunbar has the lowest rainfall and best sunshine record of any town in Scotland. The golf course is seldom, if ever, closed due to frost or snow, making it a terrific test of golf all year long. However, the local golfers say that when the wind blows a storm in, you may never be able to find the green on Whelkie Haugh.

Visitors are always welcome at Winterfield, and even if you are not able to play a round of golf, you will find that the dining room upstairs offers good meals, friendly service, and wonderful views up and down the coast.

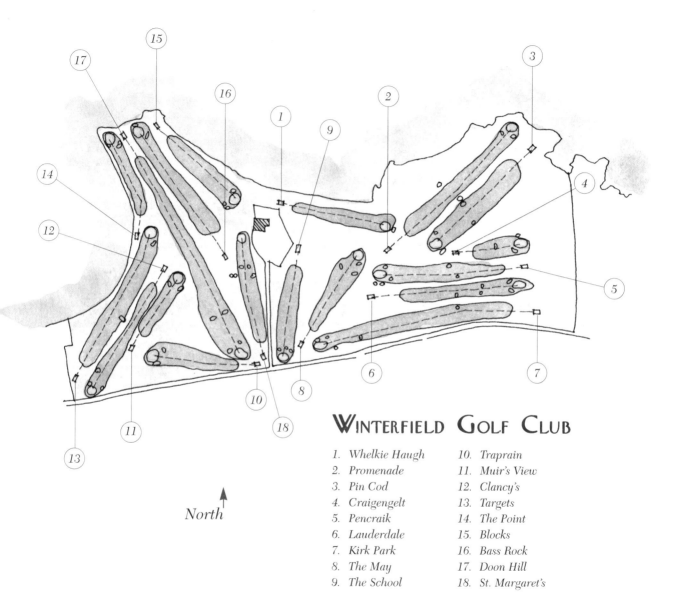

Winterfield Golf Club

1. Whelkie Haugh
2. Promenade
3. Pin Cod
4. Craigengelt
5. Pencraik
6. Lauderdale
7. Kirk Park
8. The May
9. The School
10. Traprain
11. Muir's View
12. Clancy's
13. Targets
14. The Point
15. Blocks
16. Bass Rock
17. Doon Hill
18. St. Margaret's

North

DUNBAR GOLF CLUB

*When the expense of each member for dinner amounts to two shillings
and sixpence, the Club shall be dissolved.*

One of the Regulations of the Dunbar Golfing Society—dated 1794.
(Be warned, a dinner is now considerably more than "two shillings
and sixpence.")

A historic trading port on the east coast of Scotland, thirty miles southeast of Edinburgh, Dunbar has had a turbulent history. The ruined castle overlooking the harbor attests to its role as a fortress town. John Muir, the conservationist and founder of America's national parks, is a famous son of Dunbar. The house where he was born is furnished in period style and is open to visitors.

Many Scottish and British amateur championships have been played on the links at Dunbar. Nestled along the rocky shore just northwest of St. Abb's Head, it is one of the finest links courses in all of East Lothian. Although it is not entirely clear when the game was first played at Dunbar, records show golf being played in the area as early as the beginning of the seventeenth century. In 1616 two men from the parish of Tyninghame were censured by the Kirk Session for "playing at ye nyneholis" on the Lord's Day, and an assistant minister of Dunbar was disgraced "for playing at gouff" in 1640. The Dunbar Golfing Society was established in 1794 and in 1856, after a meeting in the Town Hall, the Dunbar Golf Club was founded.

Tom Morris designed the original fifteen holes and the remaining three were added in 1880. These eighteen holes have scarcely changed since and the course is still a natural links laid out on a narrow strip of land that follows the shoreline. On the links holes the sea is always present and ready to come into play: On this course, the ball must be hit straight. Except for the 1st, 2d, 3d, and 18th holes—which are located within the walls of the old deer park that was part of the duke of Roxburghe's estate—all the holes are situated between the beach and a stone wall, which runs the full length of the course. With the engaging combination of seaside and parkland, Dunbar presents an appealing test of golf.

Dunbar Golf Club has excellent fairways, treacherous roughs, and well-manicured greens. The first two holes immediately reveal this to be a championship course. Both holes are fairly long par 5s, with a marsh to the left and rear of the first green and, at the second, strategically placed bunkers will catch any shot that is off line.

The 4th hole, Shore, begins the series of holes where the beach can come into play. At this hole, only a straight drive from the tee will keep the ball off the wall at right or out of the sea at left. Vaults, the 7th, is a par 4 whose green is located between a high stone wall and an old stone barn. The 8th, Cromwell, reminds us that Cromwell's army camped here before the Battle of Dunbar in 1650. The highest spot on the course is the tee for the 14th hole. From here, one can enjoy many splendid views either across the North Sea toward the town of Dunbar, or inland where sheep graze on the slopes of the Lammermuir Hills.

The course at Dunbar is open to all visitors.

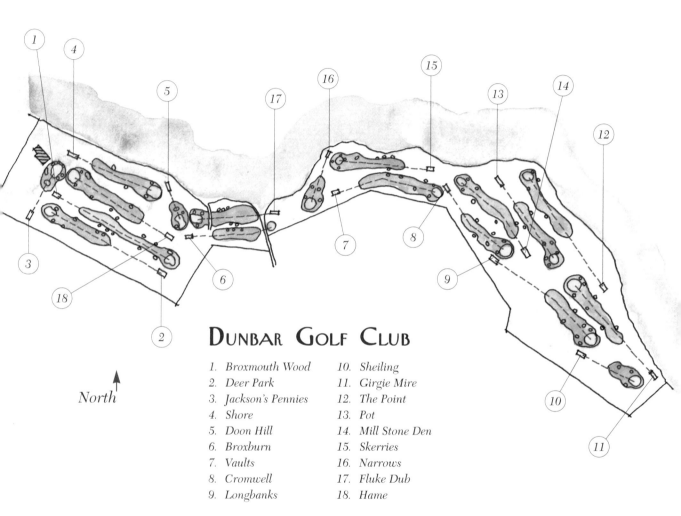

DUNBAR GOLF CLUB

1. Broxmouth Wood
2. Deer Park
3. Jackson's Pennies
4. Shore
5. Doon Hill
6. Broxburn
7. Vaults
8. Cromwell
9. Longbanks
10. Sheiling
11. Girgie Mire
12. The Point
13. Pot
14. Mill Stone Den
15. Skerries
16. Narrows
17. Fluke Dub
18. Hame

North

LONGNIDDRY GOLF CLUB

Between Edinburgh and Longniddry, one passes through Seton. Near Seton Palace, at Kirk o' Fields, Mary, Queen of Scots, is said to have played golf with the earl of Bothwell in February 1567, shortly after the murder of her second husband, Lord Darnley.

While the course at Longniddry does not boast such a colorful history, it has been the venue for several famous golf tournaments, most notably the Carling–Caledonia when both Tom Haliburton and Bernard Hunt lowered the course record to 64. In 1987, during the final qualifying round for the Open Championship held at Longniddry, the Swedish amateur Christian Hardin and English professional Peter Harrison both lowered the course record to 63, a feat later equaled by Raymond Russell, who won the Men's Open tournament at the age of 15 with a 63.

Founded in 1922, Longniddry is a superb course: part linksland, part parkland, accented with groves of Scots pines and deciduous trees. Several holes are the work of the famous course designer James Braid, and every hole has a view overlooking the Firth of Forth. The fairways are wide and lush even in the summer. The greens are fast and true, with interesting slopes that challenge the golfer; the roughs are light and well maintained. The 14th hole, Gosford, is split by two burns; the first is relatively easy to carry, but the second is placed just in front of the green to prevent an easy approach, thus making Gosford an expensive hole for the unwary. At Gorse

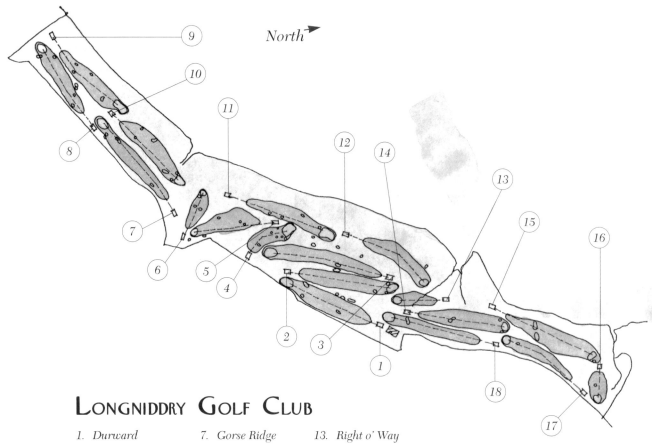

North

Longniddry Golf Club

Ridge, the 7th, the former club secretary, Mr. Osborne, overhit the green. Eventually he found his ball—sitting in a bird's nest in the bushes behind the green.

Longniddry is framed by the Firth of Forth and a shadowy woodland, one of the most picturesque courses in the area. Club members welcome visitors to their exquisite stone clubhouse, which sits on a rise looking out over the course and the Firth of Forth.

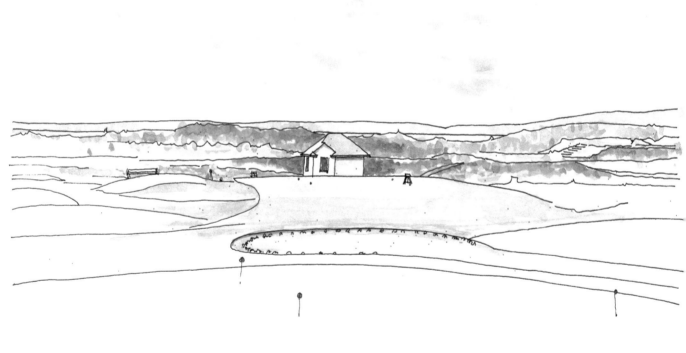

Western Gailes Golf Club

WEST OF SCOTLAND

Troon and Prestwick, old and classy
Bogside, Dundonald, Gailes, Brassie.

Prestwick St. Nicholas, Western Gailes,
St. Cuthbert, Portland—memory fails.

Troon Municipal (three links there)
Prestwick Municipal, Irvine, Ayr.

They faced the list with delighted smiles—
Sixteen courses within ten miles.

      Ancient Ayrshire golfing rhyme

Ayrshire, the home of Robert Burns, is also home to some of the finest golf courses in the world. Once described as golden links of an endless chain, Ayrshire's courses line the shore of the Firth of Clyde. This coastline boasts both spectacular rugged cliffs and golden sandy beaches. Considered the heart of golfing in the west of Scotland, Ayrshire's courses are fully exposed to the weather fronts that move in from the North Atlantic.

WESTERN GAILES
GOLF CLUB

Four golfers from Glasgow discovered this wonderful stretch of golfing country running alongside the Glasgow and South-Western Railway in 1897, when just enough room existed to sandwich the course between railway and sea. In its early days, Western Gailes was frequented most by golfers who belonged to Glaswegian clubs. They would come from the city in the morning, share the greenkeeper's small wooden shed to change and eat, then return to Glasgow by train in the afternoon.

Western Gailes is a traditional seaside links course with a line of dunes running along the right from the 5th to the 13th holes, causing the golfer always to be aware of the sea. The setting for Western Gailes is unique. The course is only two holes wide and the clubhouse is just about centrally located, which calls for play that is more like a loop than the usual out-and-back arrangement found on most courses. The defenses at Western Gailes are primarily natural. Most of the fairways are characterized by eccentric undulations, are dotted with strategically placed deep bunkers, and have beautiful, light-colored, fine-bladed links turf. It is a vast, rolling green carpet between dark green fingers of thick heather and sandhills. The tee on Sea—the 7th hole—is located on top of a sand dune by the sea, from which the golfer has magnificent views over the course to the Heads of Ayr or across the Firth of Clyde to the peaks of Arran. Wild orchids grow in the marsh near the 15th.

The greens exhibit imaginative design. Many are raised, angled, sloping platforms with narrow entrances often protected by spectacle bunkers. The 6th is hidden in a classic seaside location, and the 11th, Plateau, is a tricky hogback green. The 13th is a short hole with seven bunkers encircling the green. At the 16th, not only does the railway run alongside the fairway, a sweeping burn wraps around and defends the green.

This course has attracted numerous amateur and professional events. Harry Vardon won Western Gailes's first major tournament in 1903 with a 68—3 under par. Even though there are no ladies' tees, the Curtis Cup has been played at Western Gailes with great success.

Western Gailes is a friendly place with an elegant white clubhouse overlooking the course. Most days, the course is quiet except for the occasional train passing by.

Western Gailes is a private club that will warmly welcome visitors.

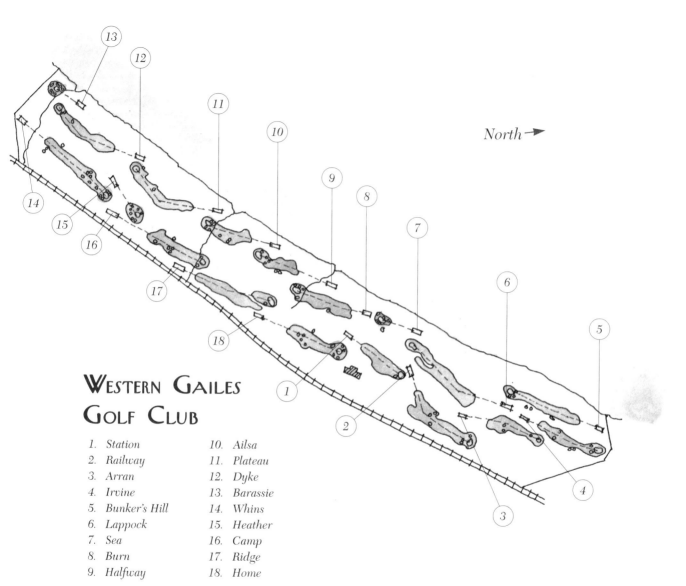

North →

WESTERN GAILES
GOLF CLUB

1. Station	10. Ailsa
2. Railway	11. Plateau
3. Arran	12. Dyke
4. Irvine	13. Barassie
5. Bunker's Hill	14. Whins
6. Lappock	15. Heather
7. Sea	16. Camp
8. Burn	17. Ridge
9. Halfway	18. Home

ROYAL TROON GOLF CLUB

The Troon club motto—*Tam arte quam marte* (As much by skill as by strength)—affirms the precise approach needed to play this course. Troon was developed in the second half of the nineteenth century as part of golf's great expansion, which began in Scotland, then spread to England, the British Empire, and the world. As at Western Gailes, the railway played an important role in the development of Troon. First, commercial interests brought wealthy merchants from Glasgow to the harbor at Troon; then they came to play golf. In 1878, a group of twenty-four men from up and down the west coast of Scotland founded the club at Troon. At first only five holes, then six, were in place. In 1883 the count had doubled to twelve and by 1888 the course had been extended to a full eighteen holes.

The course designer at Troon followed the example set at North Berwick of tees separate from the greens and built up on elevated plateaus, thus abandoning the St. Andrews pattern of tees and greens together. The course we see today is the work of Willie Fernie, the club professional in 1909. He designed the famous 8th—Postage Stamp. Originally christened Ailsa, it is a 126-yard par 3, making it the shortest hole on any British Open Championship course. The left-hand traps surrounding the green were added in 1923, on the advice of James Braid, and were situated above the level of the green. They are now positioned below the level of the putting surface. Old-timers say that the lowering of the bunkers is the result of the predicament of the German amateur, Herman Tissies, who, during the 1950 Open, took five shots to remove himself from one bunker, twelve shots to reach the green, and fifteen to hole out. Contrast this with Gene Sarazen's return to Troon in 1973 when, at the age of seventy-one, he aced this hole with a five iron. In the 1989 Open, the only stroke Greg Norman dropped in his final round of 64 was at the Postage Stamp.

In contrast, Turnberry, the par-5 6th hole, at 577 yards is the longest hole in British championship golf. As is true of most of the fairways at Troon, determining from the tee where the fairway ends and the rough begins is nearly impossible. This rugged hole is situated among the dunes where Special Service troops practiced throwing hand grenades and landing tanks on the beach during World War II.

Arnold Palmer called the 11th his pivotal hole in winning the 1962 Open Championship. This hole, The Railway—a 465-yard par 4—has been described by three-time Open Champion Henry Cotton as one of the most difficult holes in championship golf "anywhere in the world." Not one single bunker is found on the fairway, but with knee-high gorse, bracken, and heather, bunkers are not needed to cause trouble. Palmer said it has "one of the narrowest fairways I have ever laid eyes on."

From the first six holes, which follow along the beach, you can see the Peaks of Arran, the Heads of Ayr, and in the distance, Ailsa Craig. Overlooking the 17th hole is the massive Highland Marine Hotel.

This beautiful course, where the beach grass and the fairways form one continuous rolling landscape, holds an almost mystical quality. Troon held its first tournament, the Ladies' Championship, in 1904 and championships have been played ever since over the course that started out as five simple holes on Craigend Farm.

A beautiful stone clubhouse overlooks the course. Within its spacious wood-paneled rooms an air of privileged gentility reminiscent of times gone by remains. The club was granted a Royal Charter in 1978 by Her Majesty Queen Elizabeth II and since then has been known as Royal Troon Golf Club.

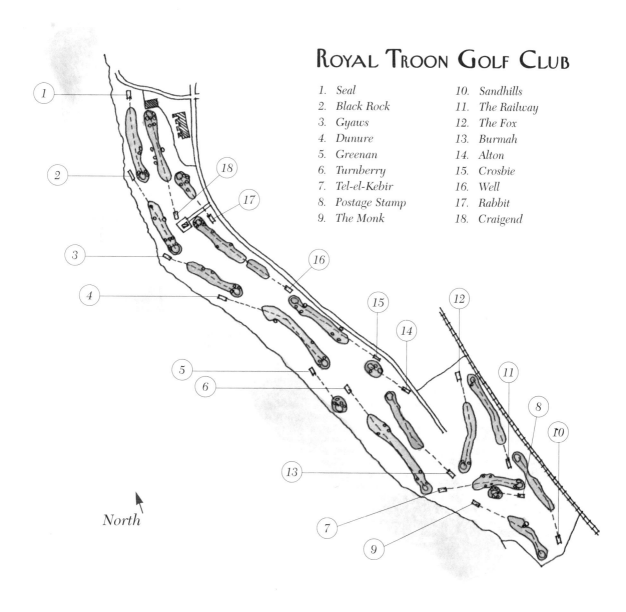

Royal Troon Golf Club

1. Seal
2. Black Rock
3. Gyaws
4. Dunure
5. Greenan
6. Turnberry
7. Tel-el-Kebir
8. Postage Stamp
9. The Monk
10. Sandhills
11. The Railway
12. The Fox
13. Burmah
14. Alton
15. Crosbie
16. Well
17. Rabbit
18. Craigend

North

PRESTWICK GOLF CLUB
OLD COURSE

Prestwick is the birthplace of championship golf. Founded in 1851, Prestwick held the first Open Championship in 1860. Willie Park from Musselburgh, a "foreigner from the east coast," beat Tom Morris by two shots over a twelve-hole course, making him the first to win what has become the world's most prestigious championship. The Open was played over the Prestwick course twenty-four times between 1860 and 1925. It is a vital course that reminds us of golf's heritage and serves as a lasting symbol to be admired and studied by golfers. It is not the quality of the course that prevents Prestwick from being a current championship venue. This ancient course lacks parking, hotel accommodations, and practice facilities, all of which are essential to staging a modern championship match.

Prestwick is the quintessential old-fashioned course: One either loves it or hates it. Full of humps and hillocks, it gives the golfer numerous controversial blind shots, which are believed by many to be the true test of golf. Such uncertainty is in the very nature of a links course. The character of the original course's twelve holes is part of the course today, with seven of the original greens still in place. The club holds an annual competition that reenacts the challenge of the original layout.

When the early Opens were held at Prestwick, they began with a whopping 578-yard first hole. Today that hole, Railway, is not nearly as long, but at 346 yards, with a stone wall on the right and deep heather and gorse on the left, it is every bit as difficult. The most famous hole at Prestwick is the 3d, Cardinal, a 500-yard par 5. Here the golfer must carry the legendary Cardinal bunker, which stretches the entire

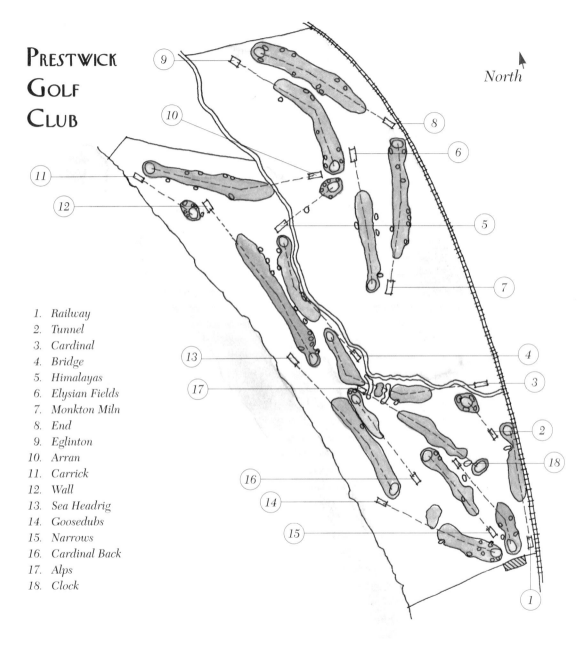

PRESTWICK
GOLF
CLUB

North

1. Railway
2. Tunnel
3. Cardinal
4. Bridge
5. Himalayas
6. Elysian Fields
7. Monkton Miln
8. End
9. Eglinton
10. Arran
11. Carrick
12. Wall
13. Sea Headrig
14. Goosedubs
15. Narrows
16. Cardinal Back
17. Alps
18. Clock

width of the fairway, right at the point of the dogleg. It took the great James Braid three attempts to dislodge his ball from the grip of this cavernous bunker with its deep, sleepered ramparts. The 4th, one of golf's first doglegs, prepares you for the infamous Himalayas, the 5th hole. This blind hole is a par 3. A small white disc near the top of a dune marks the line the ball must take to avoid five greenside bunkers. The 17th, Alps, is similar but has just one bunker, the Sahara, in front of the green. After hitting, one rushes over the hill to see if the shot was good. In 1987 the Amateur Championship was played at Prestwick on this challenging course whose rolling fairways still prove a test for the modern golfer.

Like the course, the clubhouse at Prestwick has a traditional atmosphere. Ladies are not permitted in the dining and smoking rooms, where coats and ties must be worn at all times. All are welcome in the Cardinal Room in which a fine light lunch is served. The clubhouse contains the records of some of the great events of golf. A picture on display shows a bearded Tom Morris, who was the club professional from 1851 to 1864. The scorecard signed by his son, Young Tom, when he won his third British Open in 1870 by twelve strokes is also displayed. Young Tom achieved his first Open title in 1868 when he was only seventeen, succeeding the 1867 champion, his father. He is still the youngest winner of golf's greatest contest.

The course at Prestwick is open to all visitors.

PRESTWICK
ST. NICHOLAS
GOLF CLUB

Near the mouth of the River Ayr, on a narrow strip of rolling linksland, is the 140-year-old Prestwick St. Nicholas Golf Club. Although this is not a well-known course, it is a challenging one that was used as a final qualifier for the Open Championship when it was played in Ayrshire.

The length of the course is just under six thousand yards, every yard of which is a test. The golfer will find erratic rolling fairways with numerous blind shots. Well-placed bunkers catch any mis-hit shot. The entire course is crisscrossed by stone walls and edged with thick gorse. The golfer has to play around stone buildings and keep away from a quarry. All of this is directly adjacent to the beach.

From the tees on the tops of sand dunes, one can enjoy spectacular views of the Firth of Clyde, speckled with the white sails of boats sailing from Ayr, and look across to the blue peaks on the Isle of Arran.

St. Nicholas has a fine, spacious clubhouse that overlooks the Firth of Clyde, and a friendly staff, a member of which produced an accurate, hand-drawn map of the course for us the first time we visited the club. This course is not nearly as busy as its famous neighbors and is well worth visiting, for you will find a challenging seaside course and a friendly atmosphere.

The course at Prestwick St. Nicholas Golf Club is open to all visitors.

BELLEISLE
GOLF COURSE

Even though Belleisle is not a seaside course, it has one of the finest views across the Firth of Clyde to the Isle of Arran. Belleisle, a beautiful parkland golf course with long fairways flanked by hundreds of tall, lush beech trees, is crisscrossed by a winding burn. Sprawling out over what was once a vast estate, it lives up to the challenge of its well-known neighbors. This is among the few public golf courses to stage professional tournaments.

Belleisle was designed by James Braid in 1927. The test at Belleisle comes from Braid's uncanny ability to use the natural features of the landscape and develop holes with their own unique characters. Many of the holes have long rolling fairways with either bunkers or groves of trees to catch any ball that is off line. The 2d, The Gardens (a 470-yard par 5), is a perfect example of this combination. If the sheer length does not unnerve the golfer, then the small grove of mature trees blocking the approach shot will certainly give him second thoughts. The next hole is a par 3 of daunting proportions. At 176 yards, its uphill nature makes it seem more like 280 yards and when you do reach the green you find that it is surrounded by six bunkers and a mound. This is Bunker Hill. For added excitement Ca' Canny, the 16th, has a burn crossing its fairway.

The clubhouse is a splendid stone building set in a picturesque landscape. A large pro shop, many off-course facilities, and a friendly staff eager to help all add to

BELLEISLE GOLF COURSE

1. The Ridges
2. The Gardens
3. Bunker Hill
4. Braid's Bend
5. Shanter Way
6. The Lang Drap
7. The Wee Neat
8. The Glade
9. Hirplin Hill
10. The Clay Biggan
11. Rozelle
12. The Beeches
13. Summerfield
14. Tam O'Shanter
15. Slaphouse
16. Ca' Canny
17. Curtecan
18. Brown Carrick

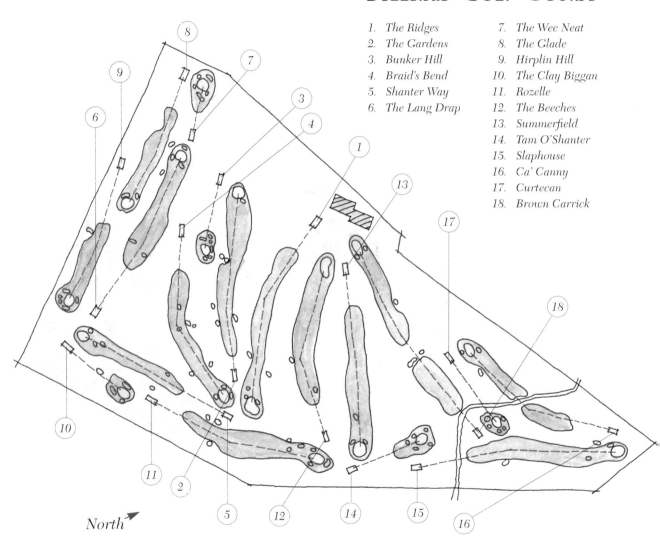

North

the enjoyment of a visit to Belleisle. After a round of golf you can visit the deer park adjacent to the course.

The course at Belleisle, which many consider the best public parkland course in Britain, is open to all visitors.

TURNBERRY HOTEL
GOLF CLUB

On wild land along the sea stretches a dramatic seaside course. The lighthouse stands on a rocky point, an ever-present reminder of the location of the sea. The Ailsa Course, set on the rugged coastline of Turnberry Bay, is a perfect vantage point from which to stand and enjoy the magnificent view across the Firth of Clyde to the towering peaks of Arran. Beyond that, one can see further to the long, low peninsula of Kintyre. Turning to the south, the massive granite outcrop of Ailsa Craig comes into view. Just out of sight, to the north, clinging to the cliffs along the coast, is the splendid Culzean Castle.

The two world wars wreaked havoc on this beautiful linksland. In World War I the Royal Flying Corps used these links as a pilot training station; in World War II, the RAF Coastal Command filled the entire area with enormous buildings and laid out a series of concrete runways.

Restoration of Ailsa and Arran—the two courses at Turnberry—began in 1946. Mackenzie Ross produced a masterpiece when he designed the Ailsa course. To show the contractor exactly the shape, size, and contour he desired, Ross made complete models of all the greens. Men happier to create a course than destroy one completed the restoration in June 1951.

Turnberry is a place of fierce competition. In the 1977 Open, during one of many championship matches played over the Ailsa course, Tom Watson and Jack Nicklaus competed in the battle known as the "Duel in the Sun." They played three identical rounds. Then, paired in the final round, Nicklaus scored a 66 and Watson won with a score of 65.

Play on Turnberry's Ailsa course becomes especially intriguing when the golfer reaches the dramatic holes. Perched on a sheer cliff, fifty feet above the beach below, is the championship tee at the 9th, Bruce's Castle, named for the Scottish king, Robert the Bruce. (The remains of his castle can be seen from the 9th green and the 10th tee.) To reach the safety of the fairway one must drive the ball two hundred yards over an inlet of the sea. The fairway is only twenty yards wide and the wind is always blowing, ready to carry your ball into a woolly rough. This is Mackenzie Ross's most challenging hole and it doesn't have—or need—a single bunker.

The tee for the 10th, Dinna Fouter, is even more theatrical. A bay of rocks and sand covers the whole of the left side and, with every hazard in full view, you must decide just how far to the right you can play and still maintain a safe distance from disaster. "Dinna Fouter" (Don't mess about) is sound advice when going for the green.

Wee Burn, the 16th, calls for decisiveness, accuracy, and courage. The "little stream" that wraps around the carpetlike green is Wilson's Burn and it is not so wee if you fail to carry it.

Turnberry is stunning when the course is quiet and the colors of the evening sky reflect across the land and the sea. From its vantage point overlooking the Irish Sea, the Turnberry Hotel provides a magnificent view as the summer sun dips behind the Isle of Arran. Originally located on the top of the hill to provide an easy point of arrival from the train, the long, red-roofed white building, reminiscent of a grand country house, maintains a turn-of-the-century tradition of elegance. Next to the Ailsa and Arran courses, a modern clubhouse contains a fine lounge and gift shop.

Turnberry welcomes visitors with a certificate of handicap. Prior arrangements must be made in writing.

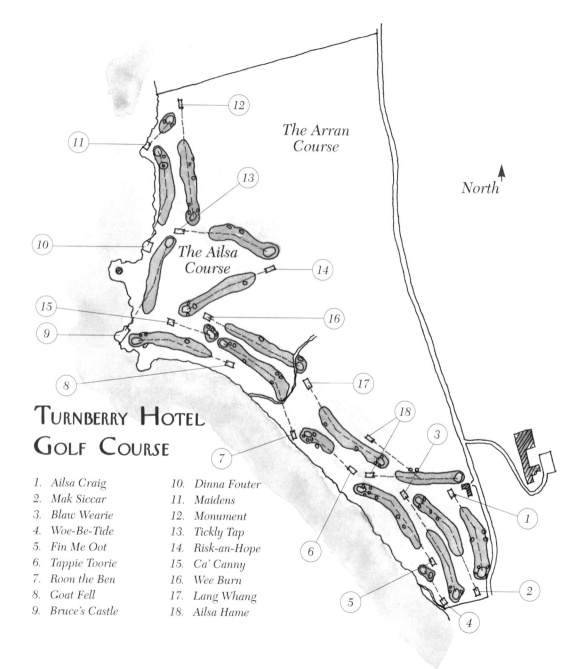

North

The Arran
Course

The Ailsa
Course

TURNBERRY HOTEL
GOLF COURSE

1. Ailsa Craig
2. Mak Siccar
3. Blaw Wearie
4. Woe-Be-Tide
5. Fin Me Oot
6. Tappie Toorie
7. Roon the Ben
8. Goat Fell
9. Bruce's Castle
10. Dinna Fouter
11. Maidens
12. Monument
13. Tickly Tap
14. Risk-an-Hope
15. Ca' Canny
16. Wee Burn
17. Lang Whang
18. Ailsa Hame

Crail—Balcomie Golf Course

FIFE

"Bid farewell to Scotland, and cross to Fife."

This ancient proverb epitomizes the relative isolation of the Kingdom of Fife from the rest of Scotland. The Romans avoided Fife, the Danes and the Norsemen only raided the coast occasionally, and the English rarely attacked it. Something about this place is infinitely soothing. Picturesque farmsteads are set on rich fertile farmland, the Firth of Forth gently laps against wide, soft, sandy beaches, and splendid harbors shelter Scotland's fishing boats. This small corner of Scotland is home to some of the world's oldest and finest golf courses.

ELIE~
THE GOLF HOUSE CLUB

Keep on hitting it straight until the wee ball goes in the hole.
—James Braid

Centuries ago, Elie was established as a Danish settlement. For three hundred years, golfers roamed over this area, hitting balls in whichever direction pleased them, making up holes as they went along. Only in 1770, when a Long and a Short course were laid out, was any order imposed upon this chaos. Even so, in those early days—when there were no clubs, subscriptions, and green fees—all were entitled and welcome simply to walk out and play. Such informality ended in 1858, when the neighboring village of Earlsferry joined Elie to establish the Earlsferry and Elie Golf Club. The membership met in the Golf Tavern or the Town Hall until 1873, when four leading members formed the Golf House Club as a means to raise funds to build a new clubhouse. The Earlsferry and Elie Golf Club disbanded in 1912, relinquishing its claim as the club at Elie to the uniquely named Golf House Club.

The Elie Golf Club Committee was a progressive group. At a time when golf courses were cropped by rabbits and sheep, the committee purchased iron bands to maintain the holes in 1874. In 1877 they purchased a lawnmowing machine for the putting greens, consuming 82 percent of the club's total income for that year. Mechanical lawnmowers would not be in general use at golf courses until about 1890.

In the 1890s, a youthful James Braid was honing his game on the links at Elie. The son of an Elie plowman who did not play golf, Braid went on to win the Open Championship five times between 1901 and 1910. He felt so strongly about the qualities of his course at Elie that he believed it could challenge the rest of the world. Other golfers have also carried the fame of Elie into the world. Douglas Rolland, Braid's cousin, is commonly considered one of the finest players never to have won the Open. Rolland was able to hit the ball farther than a ball had ever been hit before, usually with borrowed clubs.

In 1896, Tom Morris stretched the course to eighteen holes. James Braid modified it in 1921, and this is essentially the course played today. The 1st hole, Stacks, is not the easy start typically found at most seaside links: It begins with a blind drive over a very sharp rise. After looking through a vintage-1938 submarine periscope to see if the fairway is clear, the starter begins your round by stating simply, "play away." This is an invigorating start, especially when your shot carries the rise.

The first five holes are relatively quiet. Once your drive at the 6th goes over the brow of the hill, however, the course changes from rolling farmland to sweeping coastline. From the tee on the 11th, Sea Hole, you can see the coast of East Lothian across the Firth of Forth, with the Lammermuir Hills vanishing into a blue haze. On the horizon is the Isle of May, a lone sentinel in the North Sea.

James Braid described Croupie, the 13th, as "the finest hole in all the country." It follows the curve of the rocky bay and ends on a raised, angled green near McDuff's cave, carved into a mountainous cliff rising above the course.

The relaxed atmosphere belies the difficulty of the course; be prepared to meet all the seaside-course challenges. The wind can easily nudge your ball into the water or lose it in the rough.

A fine clubhouse serves as a focus for a golfing center that includes a nine-hole course, a children's course, practice grounds, and tennis courts. With white, sandy beaches, a peaceful harbor area, and the quaint village itself, Elie is the perfect place to experience a round of seaside golf.

The course at the Golf House Club in Elie is open to all visitors.

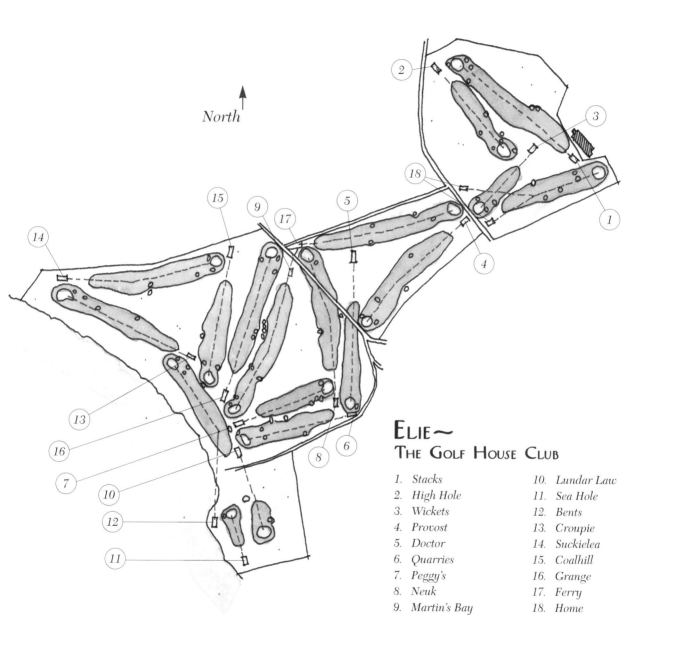

North

ELIE~
THE GOLF HOUSE CLUB

1. Stacks
2. High Hole
3. Wickets
4. Provost
5. Doctor
6. Quarries
7. Peggy's
8. Neuk
9. Martin's Bay
10. Lundar Law
11. Sea Hole
12. Bents
13. Croupie
14. Suckielea
15. Coalhill
16. Grange
17. Ferry
18. Home

CRAIL~
BALCOMIE GOLF COURSE

In 1538, Mary of Guise, bride of James V and mother of Mary, Queen of Scots, landed at Fifeness and spent her first days in Scotland at Balcomie Castle on the eastern promontory of the Fife peninsula. The seventh-oldest golf club in the world now makes its home on this most-easterly tip of the windswept East Neuk of Fife.

The founding of the club is recorded in the Crail Golfing Society's minutes, which have been kept faithfully since its first meeting: "Several gentlemen in and about the town of Crail who were fond of the diversion of Golf, agreed to form themselves into a Society. The Society was accordingly instituted upon the 23d day of February 1786." As was the custom in most golfing societies, members were required to wear the uniform of their club. In those early days, members wore scarlet jackets with bright yellow buttons, probably designed to make them more visible on the course and more conspicuous in town. They were also fined a half-mutchkin (nearly a pint) of punch for failure to turn up for a match.

In 1895, after playing on a narrow strip of land at Sauchope, which is slightly closer to the town of Crail, the club moved to its present location at Balcomie Links. Old Tom Morris had a hand in laying out this 5,720-yard par 69 course. The golfer stays within sight of the sea at every hole, and at no other course does the rocky beach come into play better than at Balcomie. When the wind blows, the distances seem farther and the line to the pin appears less attainable.

The course is always well maintained and the greens, which have a reputation for being challenging, are either slanted or contoured. The first five holes provide one of the best openings of any seaside links. Boathouse, the 1st, starts at a high tee,

CRAIL~
BALCOMIE GOLF COURSE

1. Boathouse
2. Ower the Knowe
3. The Briggs
4. Fluke Dub
5. Hell's Hole
6. North Carr
7. Breeches Buoy
8. Dykeside
9. Castle Yetts
10. The Turn
11. Lang Whang
12. The Burn
13. Craighead
14. The Cave
15. Mill Dam
16. Spion Kop
17. Road Hole
18. The Quarry

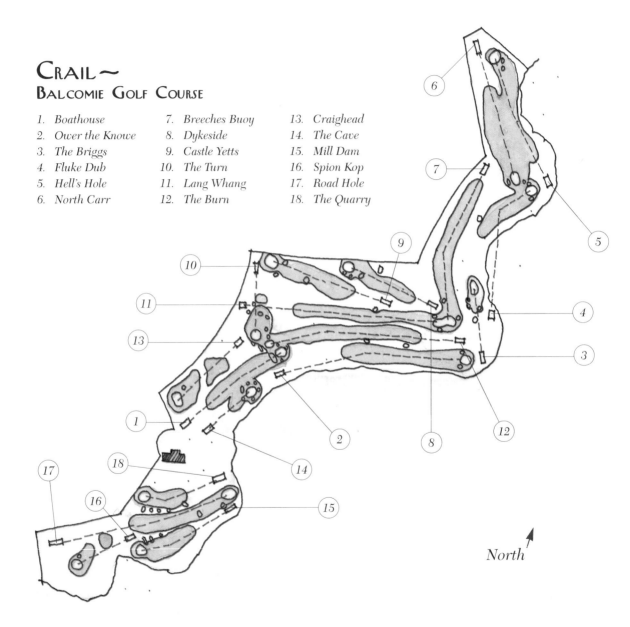

North

then descends rapidly to a well-protected green alongside an old stone boathouse. The 2d, Ower the Knowe, is a long par 5 that slips along the rocky beach. The Briggs, the 3d, is a short hole located on a small marine terrace. The 4th is a dogleg called Fluke Dub, where the golfer must drive either directly over the beach or play it safe and keep to the extreme left, which may require at least one additional shot to the hole. Hell's Hole, the 5th, skirts the rocky shoreline and requires the golfer to demonstrate straight, bold hitting. The 6th through the 14th holes all have up-and-down, well-bunkered fairways—most of which are bordered by a wall that haunts the slicer—and well-protected, rolling greens.

A path leads to a protected terrace where the last four holes are located. A sort of minicourse in themselves, these holes are open to the water on one side and surrounded by heather and thick gorse on the other three. Once you have played Balcomie's links it is easy to understand Old Tom's statement that "there is no better in Scotland."

The clubhouse, on the hill overlooking the terrace, has a commanding view of the course and a panoramic vista across the North Sea. The club atmosphere is friendly. Local golfers love their course, especially when the weather is up and the wind is blowing. It is currently being renovated to enlarge it slightly and to lengthen several of the holes. The renovation, which has received enthusiastic support, promises to continue the tradition of great golfing at Crail.

Except for a few competition days, Balcomie Golf Course in Crail is open to all visitors.

St. Andrews ~
The Old Course

*S*t. Andrews shines as a beacon illuminating the world of golf. Following this guiding light, golfers make the pilgrimage to St. Andrews in vast numbers, searching for their ultimate game. Golf has been played over these links for nearly six centuries. No other course possesses the mystique or the tradition of St. Andrews; it sets the standard for all other courses throughout the world.

By the beginning of the sixteenth century, kings and the nobility were playing golf, although just how they played it is a bit unclear. Since the links were used by footballers, archers, bowlers, shepherds, and just about anyone else who wanted to wander among the dunes and gorse, the addition of golf balls flying about must have added a certain measure of chaos to the scene.

In 1691, a professor at St. Andrews University referred to the town as "the metropolis of Golfing." With St. Andrews and its Old Course the indisputable focus, golf had become a complex and regulated sport by the middle of the eighteenth century and, by 1750, nearly every adult male in St. Andrews played the game.

Scotland experienced an upsurge in its economy following the 150 years of turmoil that attended the Scottish Reformation. The squires and lairds of Scotland now had greater wealth, increased leisure time, and the ability to travel, making it possible for them to play against others from distant areas. Golf became a serious game, which generated the need to establish a set of rules.

In 1754, twenty-two golfers from St. Andrews founded the Society of St. Andrews Golfers and adopted a set of rules nearly identical to those established by the Gentlemen Golfers of Leith in 1744. In their first meeting, the members of the new club referred to St. Andrews as "the Alma Mater of Golf" and described themselves as "being Admirers of the Anticient and Healthful Exercise of the Golf," and at the same time having "the Intrest and Prosperity of the Anticient City of St. Andrews at heart."

Prior to 1764, the Old Course comprised twelve holes. The first and last holes were played once, and the middle ten holes were played both "going out" and "coming in." (A round of golf consisted of twenty-two holes at the time.) In 1764 the first four holes were reduced to two, making the total length of the course eighteen holes. Over the next century, all golf courses accepted eighteen holes as the standard length for a complete round of golf.

As the game became increasingly popular, the arrangement of using the same hole both going out and coming in not only taxed the patience of golfers, but was just plain dangerous, causing players to dodge balls flying in from both directions. Although the fairways were widened slightly in 1832, the Old Course retains the character of the early course and still has only four holes with a single green: the 1st, 9th, 17th, and 18th.

Golf is a sport for traditionalists and this has been of the utmost importance to the citizens of St. Andrews. Even after the refinements made in 1832, the fairways remained relatively narrow, unmown, and lined with thick gorse. Any infringement on the integrity of the Old Course was cause for concern. In the early nineteenth century, a citizen of St. Andrews who attempted to raise rabbits on the links was met with the argument that golf was "extremely useful to the town" and generally considered as "a sort of necessary of life."

In 1834, eighty years after its founding, the Society of St. Andrews Golfers received the patronage of King William IV and was given a new name: Royal and Ancient Golf Club (R&A). For twenty years, the R&A met in the Union Parlor, located just east of today's eighteenth green on the Old Course. When time came to determine a site for the new clubhouse, all the old caddies were consulted, for the site could not interfere with the quality of play on the Old Course or compromise the tra-

ditions of local golf. A site at the east end of the Old Course was selected and, in 1854, one hundred years to the month after the club's founding, the Royal and Ancient Golf Club had its new clubhouse. George Rae, a local architect, designed the elegant two-story stone structure that has become the most recognized symbol of golf.

When the railway arrived in St. Andrews in 1852 it brought both fame and fortune. Providing an inexpensive means of transportation to the masses seeking to play the Old Course was an important step in turning St. Andrews into an international venue for championship golf. The tracks ran just to the south of the sixteenth fairway, and trains would stop when putting was in progress.

An artisan and service industry developed around golf, which became a business for many members of St. Andrews's working class, who became caddies, ball makers, club makers or, in some cases, all three. By the mid-nineteenth century many of these craftsmen had also become excellent golfers, two of whom are legendary: Allan Robertson and Tom Morris, Sr.

Members of Allan Robertson's family had been caddying and making golf equipment in St. Andrews for over one hundred years. He was known as the best ball maker in St. Andrews, and an even better golfer. It is widely believed that he was never defeated in competition.

Robertson's apprentice (and, later, partner), Tom Morris, Sr., a man of great character, won the Open Championship four times and became St. Andrews's most well-known figure. He became the Royal and Ancient's first professional in 1865 and cared for the Old Course until 1904. Under Morris's supervision, the quality of the greens and bunkers was greatly improved. In 1876 he devised containers of sand to use to tee the ball, thus introducing fixed tee boxes. (Wooden tees developed later in the century.) His work on the Old Course at St. Andrews defined what a golf course should be and, to a greater or lesser extent, defined what all other golf courses, whether links or parkland, ought to be.

The golfer's first image of the Old Course is of a flat, treeless strip of land, but as you play, it becomes clear that St. Andrews is truly a championship course. It is old, not feeble. The Old Course has seen twenty-four Open Championship tournaments—the most recent in 1995—played over it. Nearly all of the world's finest golfers have tested their skills against the rigors of the Old Course. A round on this course will expose the golfer to a full range of emotional experiences, which may run from one extreme to another—often on a single hole. Whereas a poor shot may seem to be proof of one's lack of attention, less-than-adequate skill, and of not being equal to the test, a good shot serves as evidence of one's worth and ability to meet the challenge.

The Old Course is a severe test of the golfer's patience, skill and, above all, character. Not all those who have played here have passed this test. For example, in 1847 the Royal and Ancient established a fine for tearing up golf cards on the course. While we can empathize with the guilty, this simple fine establishes the principle that a match is played to its completion, tangible evidence that the game is to be played with integrity as well as skill.

This course's main defenses are its bunkers and the wind. Many of the bunkers are hidden, some not much larger than a saucepan, and nearly all have evocative names—Hell, Coffin, Grave—while others are named after gallant men or those who have met with misfortune. The wind is always blowing at St. Andrews, one moment from this direction, the next from another. It has been known to blow in the golfer's face all the way around.

The first tee is squarely in front of the citadel of golf: the old, grey-stone clubhouse of the R&A, with the long, sweeping curve of St. Andrews Bay to the right. More than likely, all eyes will be on you as you tee up your ball. (After all, this *is* the Old Course.) Ahead of you lies the vast fairway that belongs to both the 1st and the 18th holes. No matter how often you stand on this tee, you will be fully aware of the tradition of which you are now a part. If all this is overwhelming, the first hole of the Old Course will help ease your anxiety. It is just about the easiest opening hole of any championship course anywhere. All you need to do is clear Swilken Burn, which twists across the fairway to protect the front of the green.

It is the second hole that will cause you to choose between courage and fear, a decision you will need to make many times during the rest of the round. A golfer can play safely to the broad side of the fairway to the left or take a straighter, albeit bolder, line down the right, which risks landing the ball in the gorse that runs the entire length of the course.

Soon you realize the open, expansive nature of the Old Course. Old-timers believe that a golfer trying to find the correct line to play is like a river pilot navigating in an open sea. Fortunately, many friendly staff patrol the course to help any golfer who becomes lost.

The fairway is hidden by a heathery bank on the 6th hole, and if you play too far to the left, the two huge Coffin bunkers lie in wait. The 7th is the only true dogleg on the course. It is defended by the enormous Shell bunker. The 8th, Short Hole, has remained the same since time beyond memory. High Hole, the 11th, is one of the world's most celebrated and challenging holes, presenting a clearly defined target and then powerfully defending it. The green is very narrow from front to back, and slopes dramatically upward before dropping off to the rugged bank that runs down to the estuary of the River Eden.

At the 13th, Hole o' Cross—a 398-yard par 4—the golfer again must deal with the ominous Coffins bunkers and, near the green lurking in the heather and gorse, the infamous Hole o' Cross bunker. With an immensely deep green, this is not an easy par.

The 14th, Long Hole, is even more treacherous. Before reaching the hog-back green, the notorious bunkers (Beardies, Benty, Kitchen, Hell, and Grave, all of which are on line to the pin) must be cleared. And the wind blows out here! This can be the most destructive hole on the course and has ruined the hopes of many when the Open is played on the Old Course.

The Road Hole, the 17th, is a 461-yard par 4 that must be dealt with before reaching home. Most golfers find this hole unnerving. Your first time on the 17th tee is sure to provide a moment of terror, for squarely between the tee and the green is the famous "Black Sheds," a structure reminiscent of the train sheds that once stood there, with ST. ANDREWS OLD COURSE HOTEL written across its face. Locals can gauge a golfer's prowess by where he aims his drive. If OLD is the line, then 240 yards is needed to clear the out-of-bounds; if ST. is the line, less than 200 yards is required. Both landing zones are over the "sheds" and not visible from the tee.

The golfer's second shot must clear the giant Scholar's bunker, which lies ready to catch any errant ball. The narrow, infamous green of the 17th is on a plateau about three or four feet above the fairway. Just to the left of center is the viciously deep Road Hole bunker biting into the green. This green has produced celebrated triumphs and devastating disasters. On a modern course, this hole would be considered unfair and such a green would not be designed. However, it exists here and must be played.

The 18th hole has the same awesome power as the 1st. The view up the fairway toward the dignified Royal and Ancient clubhouse is spectacular. Take a deep breath, aim for the clock on the clubhouse, and let your ball fly. The Valley of Sin—a wide hollow—will be your only real hazard if you drift too far to the left. Tom Morris's green on the 18th is the biggest single green on the course. As was the case when you teed off, all eyes will be on you as you sink this final putt on the Old Course. As you leave the green and walk up the steps leading to the Royal and Ancient clubhouse, it is all but impossible to refrain from looking over your shoulder, back over the course, and being engulfed by the awareness that you have just played the Old Course at St. Andrews.

The venerable Old Course has all the vitality of a modern championship course. The Royal and Ancient is the world's premier golf club and has a worldwide membership numbering nearly eighteen hundred. Since 1984, the Royal and Ancient Golf Club and the United States Golf Association have served jointly as the ruling authority for the game.

In the summer months the area around the course has the atmosphere of a festival, not that of a medieval town. With great expectations, hundreds of golfers from the far reaches of the globe arrive in St. Andrews to play the Old Course. It is a public course, open to visitors with a handicap certificate or a letter of introduction

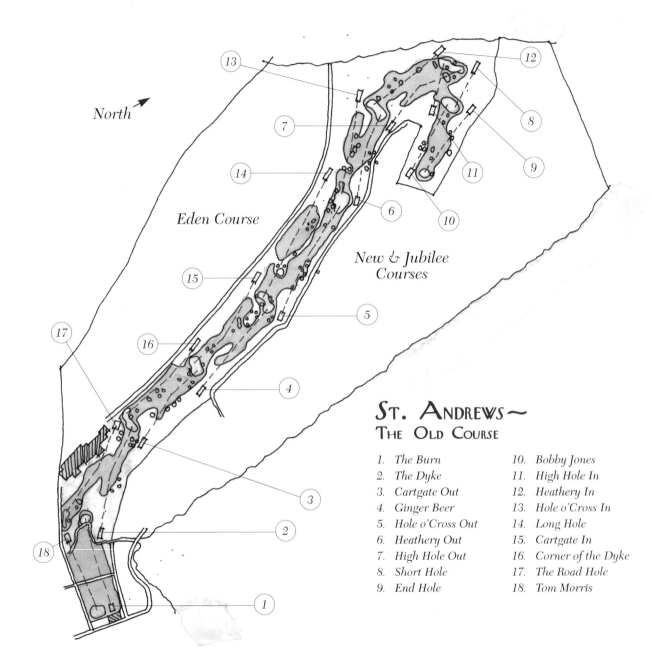

North

Eden Course

New & Jubilee
Courses

St. Andrews ~
The Old Course

1. The Burn
2. The Dyke
3. Cartgate Out
4. Ginger Beer
5. Hole o'Cross Out
6. Heathery Out
7. High Hole Out
8. Short Hole
9. End Hole
10. Bobby Jones
11. High Hole In
12. Heathery In
13. Hole o'Cross In
14. Long Hole
15. Cartgate In
16. Corner of the Dyke
17. The Road Hole
18. Tom Morris

from a golf club. Golfers wishing to reserve a tee time may do so by writing in advance, or can try their luck at the daily balloting for unreserved tee times.

When visiting St. Andrews, please remember the advice on the sign posted next to the clubhouse: DANGER—GOLF IN PROGRESS PLEASE TAKE CARE.

Panmure Golf Club

Northeast

The Picts lived in this region of Scotland around the fifth and sixth centuries. It is the land of Scotland's haunting standing stones and picturesque baronial castles. As you travel north, the coastline changes from sandy beaches to dramatic towering cliffs, where ruined medieval castles with their watchtowers look out over the North Sea. This is a place of fierce storms; more than seventy ships were wrecked along this coastline during the storm of December 1799 alone. Along this remarkable coast are some of the world's finest golf courses.

MONIFIETH GOLF LINKS

East of Dundee is Monifieth Golf Links, a classic links course. Its popularity is evidenced by the large number of clubhouses that line the edge of the course in a manner that suggests beachfront property more than a golf course. Traditionalists love Monifieth. Its fairways are narrow with many unpredictable blind shots; deep bunkers await any ball from a miscalculated shot; and the railway serves as the out-of-bounds for the first six holes of the course.

Seafaring folk who relished strenuous battles against nature were among the first to take up golf. To the sailor, a "fairway" was a navigable channel to a safe harbor. A sailor invented the first golf bag, using canvas from sails, and the present-day "Sunday Bag" is not too different from the original. The elected leader of each club is not called its president, but its captain. During one of the early championships played at St. Andrews a sudden storm blew in and interrupted play. Maitland Dougall was just about to tee off when the storm broke and a ship out on the bay began to founder. Dougall left the match immediately, spent the next five hours in a lifeboat rescuing the crew, then returned, continued his game, and won the title. The presence of a ship's mast near the first tee of every links is a vivid reminder of the nautical influence on the early development of golf, so it's not surprising to see one rising above the trees near the first tee at Monifieth.

Most of the fairways at Monifieth are lined with trees, a feature not usually found on links courses. Sometimes these block the wind and make play easier, but at other times the trees channel the wind and make the flight of the ball absolutely

unpredictable. With its combination of trees and sandhills, Monifieth is a challenging course. The highly regarded 16th, Wilderness, while situated in the rolling dunes, is also surrounded by trees. You feel as if you really are in the wilderness, for only the bunkers remind you of the task at hand.

The course at Monifieth has staged the Scottish Amateur Championship and is a favorite among the area's golfers, who take great pride in its unusual characteristics. Golfers often feel as if they have this quiet course to themselves.

The course at Monifieth is open to all visitors.

Panmure Golf Club

Before winning the 1953 Open Championship at Carnoustie, Ben Hogan practiced at the course at Panmure, spotlighting the true potential of the Panmure Golf Club's course. Although not as famous as Carnoustie, its neighbor to the northeast, Panmure commands a golfer's respect.

The course has two moods. The beginning and end of the course are more pastoral, while the middle section is within a stone's throw of the North Sea. The entire course is covered with odd-looking little hillocks blanketed with heather—not quite the size of dunes but equally menacing. After the short 5th, the terrain changes on the far side of a dense little pine woods. The 6th, with a plateau green raised above those curious hillocks, was described by Hogan as one of the finest holes he'd seen. For most golfers, the next series of holes, with rumpled fairways and a never-ending sea of mounds, is the most difficult section of the course. At the 12th, a winding burn protects the front of an elevated green, while mounds trap any overshot. From the 16th to the finish, the course returns to its flatter nature, but this area sports little elbow room and a deep rough edging the fairway.

A picturesque white cottage framed by trees—the Panmure Golf Club clubhouse—comes into view as you play toward home. Inside this beautiful clubhouse are handsome paneled rooms, all of which look out over the course. Panmure is first and foremost a members' club. However, it offers visitors a nice selection of light meals and refreshments.

The course at Panmure is open to all visitors.

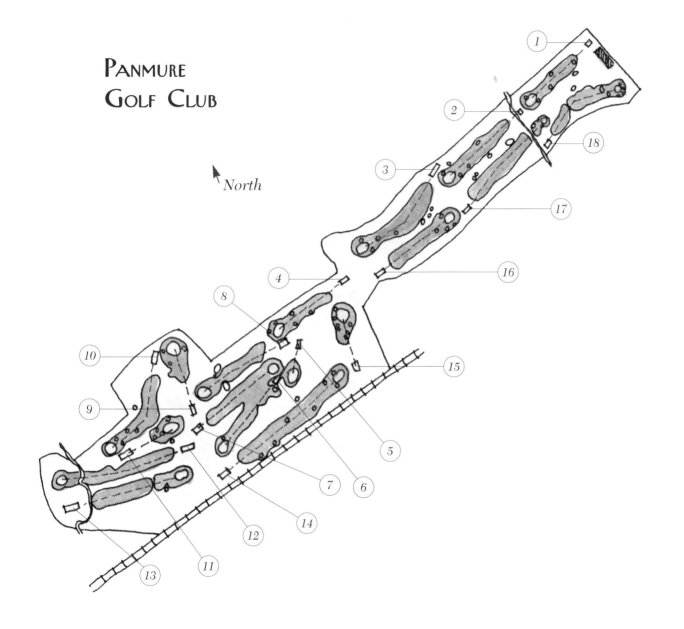

PANMURE
GOLF CLUB

North

Carnoustie
Golf Links

Although Parish records from 1560 show that "gowff " was played on the Barry Links (land adjacent to the present course) during a time when the Highlands clans were busy fighting each other, Carnoustie only began to rise in prominence during the early years of the reign of Queen Victoria (1837–1901). In 1842 the Carnoustie Golf Club was founded and the oldest ladies' golf club in the world, Carnoustie Ladies, was established in 1873. About 1850, St. Andrews's professional Allan Robertson, regarded as the finest golfer of his time, laid out the first ten holes at Carnoustie. Old Tom Morris extended the course to eighteen holes in 1867 and it was over this new course that his son Young Tom beat all comers in his debut performance at the British Open at the age of sixteen.

The famous James Braid is responsible for the present course. His modernization in 1926 was so successful that Carnoustie was able to stage its first Open Championship five years later in 1931, when Tommy Armour won with a fine closing-round score of 71.

Following the success of that first Open, James Wright, chairman of the Carnoustie Golf Courses Committee, made a visionary move and set out to improve and extend the course again. He eliminated the bunkers and other hazards, which were becoming obsolete as newly developed steel-shafted equipment came into use. Wright stated his goal for the new course: "We do not attach much importance to length as such. Quality rather than pure length has been our objective." Once again, improvements resulted in Carnoustie hosting an Open Championship in 1937.

Carnoustie has gusting wind, rolling dunes, and winding burns. Despite Wright's disclaimer, its most impressive challenge is its length. From the championship tees, it is a massive 7,335 yards long and, from the club medal tees, a formidable 6,936 yards. Every yard must be played carefully, for Carnoustie's defenses know no weaknesses. No more than two holes face in the same direction and each hole has its own unique characteristics.

Our son remembers this course as the one where golfers are always fishing their balls out of the water. A ball can be in the water at no fewer than thirteen locations. Often the golfer finds Barry Burn, Jockie's Burn, or some other small, unnamed stream running alongside or crossing the fairway. Water is often situated in front of the greens or exactly in the ideal landing zone for a key shot.

From the very first tee, the golfer will immediately recognize this as a classic links course, full of blind shots and unforeseen hazards. The infamous Barry Burn crosses forty yards in front of the tee and then, to intimidate further, runs along the left side of the fairway. A white marker above and behind the green is the only clue to where one aims a shot from the tee. In the undulating fairway rising away from the tee, no bunkers are in sight—but no fewer than nine are out there, waiting. As the name of the hole—Cup—indicates, the green lies in a hollow enhanced by a ridge at the back and right side of the green. The fairway of the 2d is in a narrow valley with Braid's bunker in the center, flanked by supporting bunkers. At the 3d, Jockie's Burn runs in front of the green within ten yards of the putting surface. If the wind is blowing, this can be a very difficult beginning.

Long, the 6th hole, is demanding, competitive, and Carnoustie's longest hole at 575 yards. Two hundred yards out from the medal tees and in the center of the fairway are two very large, deep bunkers, one directly behind the other. Just to the left, between the pair of bunkers and the out-of-bounds, is Hogan's Alley, a narrow strip of fairway named for Ben Hogan's legendary play in the 1953 Open. If you are able to exercise absolute control from the tee, this is the perfect place to take your second shot. The par-5 6th is an extremely powerful test of both the golfer's wits and skill.

The 10th, South America, is named for a local citizen who set out to take golf to the New World and, after a few too many for the road, was found next morning in the woods bordering the 10th. He was very lucky indeed not to have drowned in Barry Burn, which wraps around the front of the green, or broken his leg by falling into any of the eleven deep bunkers that defend this hole.

Many championship golfers have been victims of the sting of Carnoustie's tail. The 16th, Barry Burn, at 250 yards, is an exceptionally long par 3. Even a first-class player may need to use a driver to reach the green, which is like an upside-down saucer, built up in the center and falling away in all directions. To make matters worse, the green is surrounded by bunkers and its surface is contoured just enough to prevent the ball from rolling true.

After surviving the 16th, the golfer faces the climax of this great course. The challenge of the 17th is to stay out of Barry Burn as it twists and swirls in front of the tee and then runs diagonally from left to right across most of the fairway. From the tee the golfer must reach the island sanctuary, a section of fairway formed by a loop of the burn. A successful shot here guarantees an excellent lie and stance for a second shot. With its green protected by a series of deep bunkers, Island is an outstanding par 4, but many days the wind blowing in from the sea greatly diminishes prospects for a par.

The 18th, Home, is the final test of the golfer's nerve. Barry Burn continues to present the main obstacle, and it is now supported by three strategically placed bunkers. Johnny Miller's bunker is the largest of the three and the closest to the green. After failing his first attempt to get out of this bunker, Miller hit a most extraordinary shot that carried the burn and landed just short of the green. Local golfers remember this as the finest shot of the 1975 Open. This final hole is an exciting finish to a great golf course.

Because Carnoustie lacked a large hotel, easy access to the course, and the other nongolfing requirements necessary to support an Open Championship tournament, the Open hadn't been held here since 1975. Thanks to the tireless work of those holding the belief that Carnoustie is a course with no equal, the Open Championship will once again be held over the links at Carnoustie in 1999. Many avid golfers are delighted to see this venerable course rejoin the Open Championship rotation.

All six of Carnoustie's golf clubs welcome visitors. Each has the usual amenities for a visiting golfer as well as fine exhibits of trophies and golfing memorabilia.

The course at Carnoustie is open to all visitors.

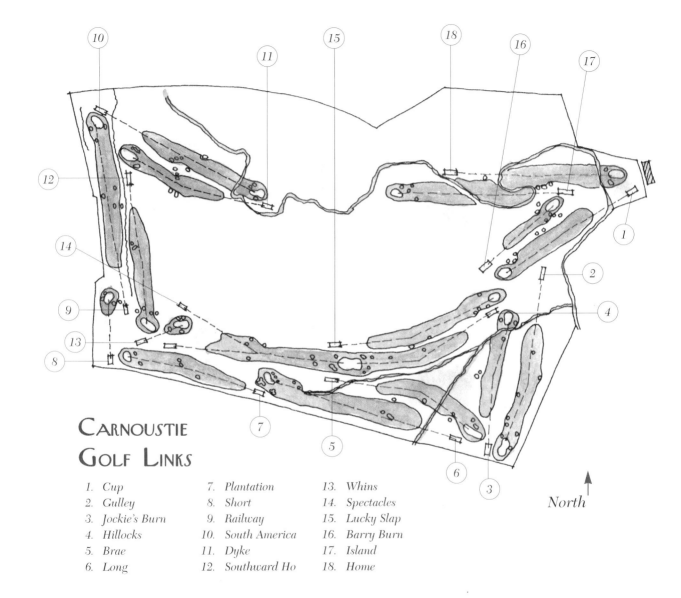

CARNOUSTIE
GOLF LINKS

1. Cup	7. Plantation	13. Whins
2. Gulley	8. Short	14. Spectacles
3. Jockie's Burn	9. Railway	15. Lucky Slap
4. Hillocks	10. South America	16. Barry Burn
5. Brae	11. Dyke	17. Island
6. Long	12. Southward Ho	18. Home

North

MONTROSE
LINKS TRUST

Along Scotland's east coast, halfway between Dundee and Aberdeen, lies the ancient town of Montrose. Nestled in mountainous dunes at the northern edge of this once-prosperous seaport is the fifth-oldest golf course in the world. James Melville, whose diaries chronicle his youth in Montrose and his student days at St. Andrews University, recorded that, as a six-year-old, he learned several sports, including golf. Since he was born in 1556, we know that golf was played in Montrose by 1562.

Montrose golfers have rallied to protect their course twice. A citizen leasing land from the town council plowed up part of the common links in 1785, provoking the town's golfers to send a protest to the sheriff deputy. In 1810, they joined to form the first Montrose golf club, thus preventing the council from constructing a new school building on the course. Both times, they defended their beloved course successfully.

At a time when some of Scotland's important golf courses had as few as 5 holes, the Montrose course had a record 25. Not all were played on every occasion, but in 1866 a unique exception occurred when an Open Championship was played over all 25 holes. Willie Park of Musselburgh, winner of the first Open in 1860, shot 115 to finish second. (The Musselburgh golf course was one of those with but 5 holes at the time.) The then-current Open Champion, Andrew Strath from Prestwick, and Jamie Anderson, a young man from St. Andrews (who would go on to win the Opens in 1875, 1876, and 1877), both shot 119. The winner of this unique event was Mr. T. Doleman from Glasgow, who won the £10 first prize by playing the 25 holes in 112 strokes.

At first glance, the only evidence that a golf course lies hidden in those mountainous dunes is the pro shop standing alongside the tee for the first hole. The giant dunes, called sandhills by local golfers, are thirty feet high with deep ravines. This wild, undulating landscape is overgrown with marram, a dense beach grass. Wind whipping over the dunes can cause even the most experienced golfer to pause. The present course dates from the early part of this century and owes much to the design work of Tom Morris and Willie Park, Jr. Twelve of the holes parallel the sea and follow the dunes, and two of these run along a clifftop that soars above the beach below. The middle holes loop out onto a flat area that provides a dramatic contrast to play in the rolling dunes; here the fairways are lined by Scotland's infamous, thick, dense gorse.

Montrose's knobbly mounds, blind shots, revetted bunkers, pulpit greens, and the ever-present, bracing sea breezes make for rugged golfing. Three holes are especially memorable. Hole 3, Table, has an unforgiving, twenty-foot-high raised green that can ruin any hope for par. In the heart of the giant dunes, Sandy Braes, the 6th hole, delivers the best panorama of the coast and across the course. Along with this breathtaking view, a steep cliff runs along the entire right side of the fairway, dropping straight to the beach below. Rashie's, the 17th—a long, difficult par 4—is often described as needing three good shots to reach the green in two.

The Medal Course at Montrose presents a challenge in the very best tradition of Scottish links golf. Many important events have been held here, including the Scottish Professional and Amateur championships, and the British Boys Championship.

The burgh of Montrose itself is a picturesque town set on a peninsula between the North Sea and Montrose Basin, where rare, pink-footed Arctic geese winter. Montrose has many fine old houses built by wealthy merchants and sea captains, a maritime museum, and one of the nicest sandy beaches along the coast.

The Montrose courses are public links, and all three clubhouses—the Royal Montrose Golf Club, Mercantile Golf Club, and Caledonia Golf Club—welcome visitors. Adjacent to the Medal course is the Broomfield auxiliary course, laid out in the 1920s.

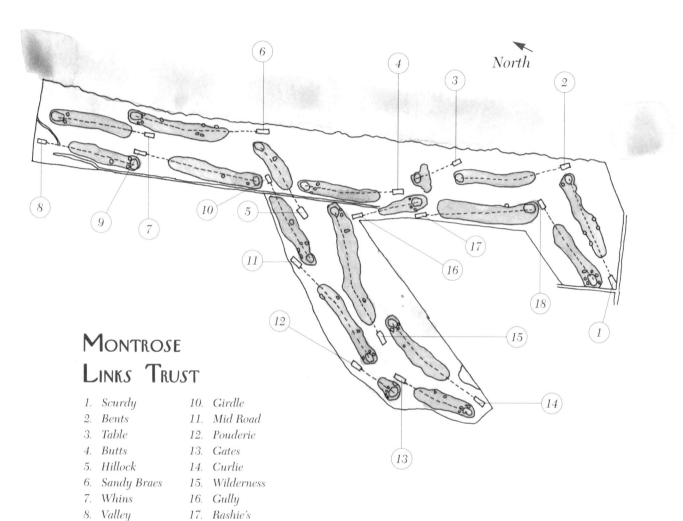

MONTROSE
LINKS TRUST

1. Scurdy
2. Bents
3. Table
4. Butts
5. Hillock
6. Sandy Braes
7. Whins
8. Valley
9. Jubilee
10. Girdle
11. Mid Road
12. Pouderie
13. Gates
14. Curlie
15. Wilderness
16. Gully
17. Rashie's
18. Dean's Drive

North

Royal Dornoch Golf Club

HIGHLANDS

In this land of clans, red deer, and golden eagles, Celtic mists cloak the majestic, rugged mountains that frame this legendary landscape, a rare mixture of awesome splendor and serene tranquillity. The Highlands were virtually inaccessible during much of Scotland's history and, except for the occasional castle, this vast landscape is mostly uninhabited. The golf courses situated among windswept dunes and wild seascapes constantly remind us of the game's seaside origins. In the Highlands, summer twilight never really gives way to nightfall and golf can be played until midnight.

CRUDEN BAY
GOLF CLUB

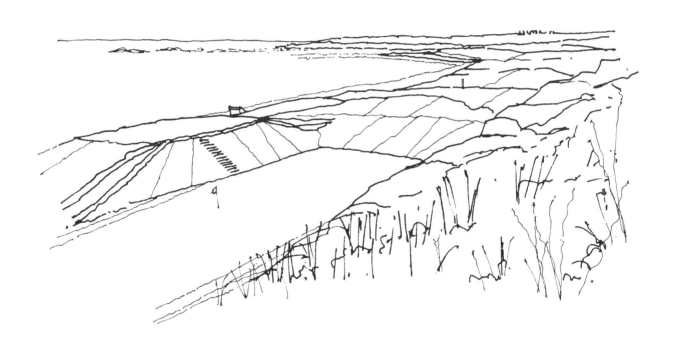

Cruden Bay is true linksland with plenty of burns to cross, hills to carry, hidden dells to drop into, and blind shots to remind us of what a round of golf was like when it was played mostly on ribbons of sandhills wedged between the sea and the more fertile soil inland. This is golf as traditionally played on a natural seaside landscape.

The remote location and seclusion of Cruden Bay make this links course special. Golfers often feel as though they have the course to themselves. Even if other players are sharing the course, the dunes ingeniously hide one hole from another. After finishing play on the 15th hole, players ring a bell placed atop the hill to signal to following golfers that the green is clear. Golf-course architect Tom Simpson is the mastermind of this impressive course.

The course's unusual form—a figure eight—allows the golfer to play along the sea as well as inland, both going out and coming in. A breathtaking panorama across the sea entices the golfer from every hole. At 6,370 yards, the course is fairly short, but it requires accuracy in every shot. Any errant ball will find itself in thick gorse, very heavy rough, or on the beach. The 8th is one of Simpson's favorites. He described this hole, which is surrounded by high dunes, as "mischievous, subtle and provocative." The beach runs along the right of the 14th, while a hill covered with thick gorse is on the left. The green itself is hidden in a dell, completely out of sight. The course is at its narrowest at the 15th—Blin' Dunt (blind shot). Its name says it all.

Cruden Bay is fun to play, for it tests the golfer's wits. If the wind is blowing, as it most surely will be, one's nerves may also be tested.

The present-day clubhouse, with its commanding view over Cruden Bay, is magnificently appointed and has the kind of warm, friendly atmosphere often found in this part of the world. Meals are served throughout the day and casual dress is permissible at all times. With all of these fine qualities it is no wonder that Cruden Bay is among the top fifty golf courses in the British Isles.

The course at Cruden Bay is open to all visitors.

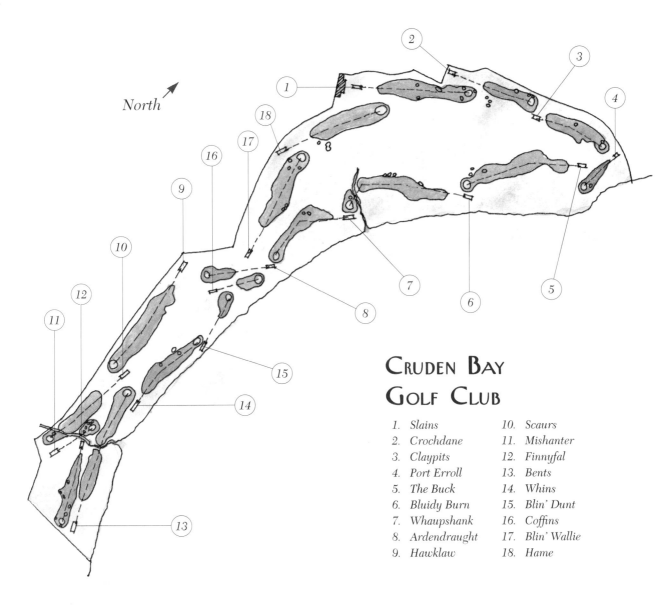

North

CRUDEN BAY
GOLF CLUB

1. Slains	10. Scaurs
2. Crochdane	11. Mishanter
3. Claypits	12. Finnyfal
4. Port Erroll	13. Bents
5. The Buck	14. Whins
6. Bluidy Burn	15. Blin' Dunt
7. Whaupshank	16. Coffins
8. Ardendraught	17. Blin' Wallie
9. Hawklaw	18. Hame

Nairn Golf Club

The course at Nairn sits in a sheltered spot along Moray Firth. Nairn has an exceptional reputation both at home and abroad. Founded in 1887, the Nairn Golf Club has hosted both the men's and ladies' Scottish Amateur Championships and recently staged the British Amateur Championship, the oldest national golf event in the world.

The original course was designed in 1887 by Archie Simpson, one of Elie's well-known golf professionals, and modified by Old Tom Morris in 1890. The present course owes its character to the work of another distinguished Elie professional, James Braid, and several new tees were built for the 1994 British Amateur Championship, which lengthened the course to 6,722 yards.

Nairn is a traditional seaside links with the opening holes running right along the shoreline. "There is no more attractive first tee in all Scotland," the Scottish golf writer Sam McKinlay stated after playing at Nairn. If a golfer's opening drive is not as good as Sam's, however, the result may be slicing into the sea on six of the first seven holes. Even though your attention is on the shoreline, you must keep a watchful eye on the ever-present gorse and heather and avoid many well-positioned bunkers as well. For example, Braid's bunker lies in wait—a menacing bunker on the 5th that will trap any shot made too far left in an attempt to avoid the beach at the right.

While the beach keeps the golfer wary on the beginning holes, the burns crossing in front of the greens on the 16th and 17th remind the golfer that it is not

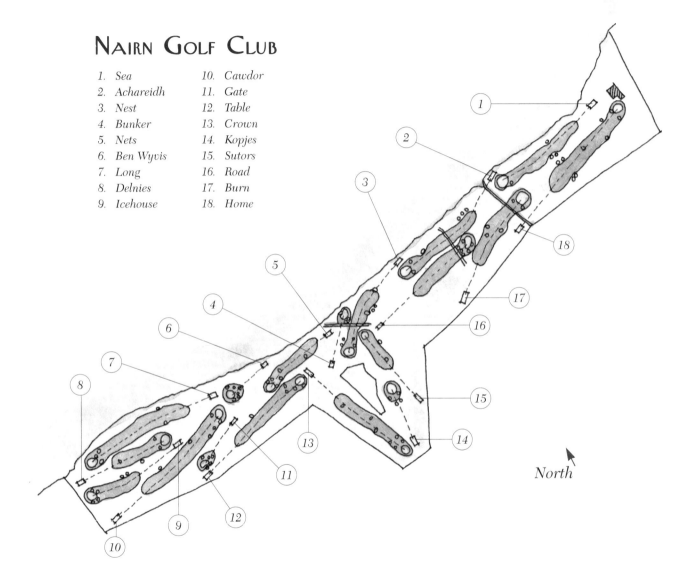

NAIRN GOLF CLUB

1. Sea
2. Achareidh
3. Nest
4. Bunker
5. Nets
6. Ben Wyvis
7. Long
8. Delnies
9. Icehouse
10. Cawdor
11. Gate
12. Table
13. Crown
14. Kopjes
15. Sutors
16. Road
17. Burn
18. Home

North

time to relax. Regardless of the season, the greens at Nairn are the finest putting surfaces in the north.

The clubhouse at Nairn is one of the newest in Scotland, with an atmosphere that is relaxed and friendly. The club has a nine-hole course on which a family can enjoy a round of golf. Known for its sandy beaches, good weather, numerous museums, and many other attractions, Nairn is an ideal place to get away from it all and experience a fine round of seaside golf.

The course at Nairn is open to all visitors.

ROYAL DORNOCH GOLF CLUB

We walk along the beach and look back over our shoulders to see the sun glistening on Dornoch links, the most northerly first-class golf course in the world. Golf has been played over this natural and endlessly varied seaside terrain since 1570. St. Andrews (1552) and Leith (1593) are the only courses to precede Dornoch (1616) in nurturing the beginning of golf in Scotland. In 1630, Sir Robert Gordon described the links at Dornoch as the fairest and largest of any in Scotland, and it is still widely regarded as one of the great Scottish courses.

Founded in 1877, the Royal Dornoch Golf Club is fairly new as clubs go. In 1886 Old Tom Morris was invited to lay out a fully planned golf course following the instructions of the founding fathers to build a course of first-class quality. Old Tom, the veteran championship golfer, redesigned the existing nine holes and planned an extension to eighteen holes, which was completed three years later. Using Dornoch links's unique natural golfing terrain, he created intriguing plateau greens. In 1906, by gracious permission of King Edward VII, the title and dignity of "Royal" was bestowed on the club.

In those early days, a number of great players were attracted to Dornoch, including J. H. Taylor, James Braid, Harry Vardon, and Harold Hilton. In more recent years, Ben Crenshaw, Tom Watson, Greg Norman, and Nick Faldo have all played over the superb course at Dornoch.

Before emigrating to the United States in 1898, Donald Ross, the son of a Dornoch stonemason, was the first golf professional and head greenkeeper at Dornoch links. Ross acquired his skills through his association with Old Tom Morris and other southern professionals at St. Andrews. American golfer Richard Tufts discovered Ross and persuaded him to leave Dornoch and take a commission to play and teach golf as a specialist at Oakley Club, just outside Boston. At the age of twenty-five, Ross arrived in America with two dollars in his pocket. Putting his ability, good education, and high standard of efficiency to use, he was employed as a pro in Pinehurst, North Carolina, by 1900. James Tufts commissioned Donald Ross to design Pinehurst No. 2, which is, beyond doubt, among the finest courses in the world. Always faithful to what he had learned at Dornoch, Ross went on to design over six hundred golf courses.

The present championship course at Dornoch is an excellent example of a modern links. Nothing is hidden; there are no blind shots. Golfers are rewarded for following the basic arts of the game . . . and punished for betraying them. The links take advantage of Dornoch's abundant natural resources. Because the course has more changes in level than most other seaside links, one's feeling of expansiveness is enhanced. That and the ever-present sea combine to help the golfer feel secluded and far from the rigors of everyday life. However, even when the wind isn't sweeping across the Moray and Dornoch firths or thundering down from the hills, the links at Dornoch can be a "smiler with a knife," as local golfers put it.

Like St. Andrews, Dornoch starts and finishes in town. The first three holes are not only memorable, they are good indications of what is to follow. The golfer immediately encounters vast rolling fairways, exquisite raised tees, and finely manicured plateau greens. An enormous bank of gorse dominates the left side of the first eight holes. We once heard a golfer remark at the 4th tee that the round was going pretty well as he had lost only five balls in the gorse so far. The 4th, one of Dornoch's finest holes, requires the golfer to navigate a humpbacked fairway to reach an exten-sive plateau green that is raised out of a hollow. The greens at Dornoch are higher than is typical on a seaside links course, and this exaggerated height makes them appear smaller than they actually are. These are the greens Donald Ross loved and emulated in other courses.

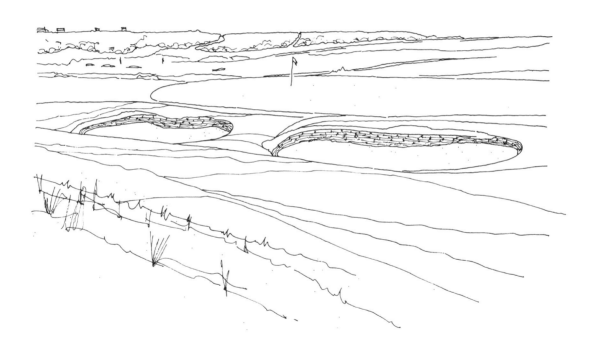

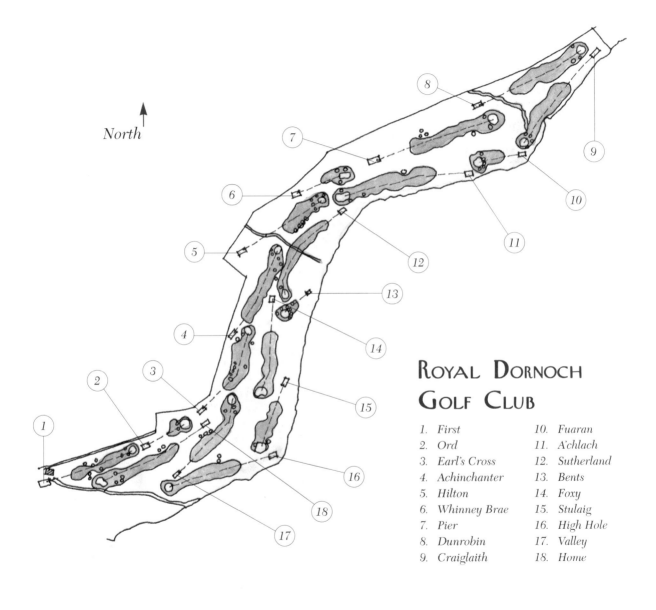

North

ROYAL DORNOCH
GOLF CLUB

1.	First	
2.	Ord	
3.	Earl's Cross	
4.	Achinchanter	
5.	Hilton	
6.	Whinney Brae	
7.	Pier	
8.	Dunrobin	
9.	Craiglaith	

10.	Fuaran
11.	A'chlach
12.	Sutherland
13.	Bents
14.	Foxy
15.	Stulaig
16.	High Hole
17.	Valley
18.	Home

After running along ridges, keeping off the beach, staying out of the gorse, and mastering those tricky elevated greens, we arrive at the 14th, Foxy—Dornoch's best-known hole—a double dogleg to a classic Dornoch raised green. Even though there are no bunkers on this hole it still requires the cunning of a fox to make par.

The 9th through the 16th holes are along the beach. At the 17th, the course reverses direction, then reverses again, back toward the clubhouse, at the 18th. Every hole requires the player to find the correct line; in fact, every square inch of the course challenges the golfer's skill. As the course guide states, at Dornoch the golfer "should never forget that there is more art than science to golf."

The course at Dornoch is open to all visitors.

Course Information

Many courses require nonmembers to make advance arrangements prior to visiting, and it is always advisable to contact the club secretary in advance, preferably in writing. You may then inquire as to the current green fees and exactly which days and times visitors are allowed to play. When booking a tee time, you may also wish to request a caddie. (On a links course, a caddie can be a valuable resource.) In some cases, a letter of introduction or a handicap certificate is required, and a few courses require that a visitor be a member of another recognized club.

Several courses listed have second and sometimes third courses adjacent to their medal courses. These courses are usually less restrictive about visitors and may be less expensive as well.

The following guidelines will help you abide by local customs when golfing in Scotland:

- Respect members-only areas.
- Remove your hat when entering the clubhouse.
- Avoid practice swings on the tee.
- Respect restricted areas.
- Women should be mindful of men-only areas.
- Golf carts are not usually available, and should not be expected.
- Play "Ready Golf," and play in less than four hours, even in a foursome.
- Take the time to stop and appreciate that you are playing on some of the best courses in the world.

Key for Green Fees

Expensive:	£40 and up
Moderate:	£25 to £40
Inexpensive:	£25 or less

All courses listed are eighteen-hole courses. Course information is arranged in the same course sequence as the text.

East Lothian

North Berwick — North Berwick West Links
West Links, Beach Road
North Berwick, East Lothian EH39 4BB
Tel: (01620) 895040
Fax: (01620) 893274
Location: A1 from Edinburgh; A198 at
    Meadowmill roundabout
Course length: 6,420 yards (white stakes)
Par: 71
Access: Visitors welcome most times
Advance contact: Required
Documents: Handicap certificate or letter of
    introduction recommended
Green fees: Moderate

Dunbar — Winterfield Golf Course
Winterfield Golf Club
St. Margaret's House
North Road

Dunbar, East Lothian EH42 1AU
Tel: (01368) 865119
Location: 1.5 miles off A1 toward Dunbar
Course length: 5,155 yards (white stakes)
Par: 65
Access: Visitors welcome most times
Advance contact: Recommended
Documents: Not required
Green fees: Inexpensive

DUNBAR — DUNBAR GOLF CLUB
East Links
Dunbar, East Lothian EH42 1LT
Tel: (01368) 862317
Location: On Seashore, .5 mile east of Dunbar
Course length: 6,426 yards (white yards)
Par: 71
Access: Visitors welcome most times
Advance contact: Required
Documents: Not required
Green fees: Moderate

LONGNIDDRY — LONGNIDDRY GOLF CLUB
Links Road
Longniddry, East Lothian EH32 0NL
Tel: (01875) 852228
Fax: (01875) 853371
Location: 18 miles east of Edinburgh, at
    Longniddry village
Course length: 6,219 yards (white yards)
Par: 68
Access: Visitors welcome midweek
Advance contact: Required
Documents: Handicap certificate required
Green fees: Moderate

WEST OF SCOTLAND

GAILES — WESTERN GAILES GOLF CLUB
Gailes
Irvine, Ayrshire KA11 5AE
Tel: (01294) 311649
Fax: (01294) 312312
Location: 2 miles southwest of Irvine
Course length: 6,639 yards (white stakes)
Par: 71
Access: Visitors welcome except Thursday and
    Saturday
Advance contact: Recommended
Documents: Handicap certificate or letter of
    introduction required
Green fees: Expensive

TROON — ROYAL TROON GOLF CLUB
Craigend Road
Troon, Ayrshire KA10 6EP
Tel: (01292) 311555
Fax: (01292) 318204
Location: .5 mile south of town center, off
    South Beach Esplanade
Course length: 6,641 yards (medal yards)
Par: 71
Access: Visitors welcome Monday, Tuesday, and
    Thursday
Advance contact: Required
Documents: Handicap certificate required
Green fees: Expensive

PRESTWICK — PRESTWICK GOLF CLUB: OLD COURSE
2 Links Road
Prestwick, Ayrshire KA9 1QG
Tel: (01292) 77404
Fax: (01292) 447255
Location: Adjacent to railway station
Course length: 6,544 yards
Par: 71
Access: Visitors usually allowed weekdays
Advance contact: Required
Documents: Handicap certificate or letter of introduction required; visitors must be members of another recognized club
Green fees: Expensive

PRESTWICK — PRESTWICK ST. NICHOLAS GOLF CLUB
Grangemuir Road
Prestwick, Ayrshire KA9 1SN
Tel: (01292) 77608
Location: On seafront, 1 mile south of town center, off Ayr Road
Course length: 5,952 yards (white yards)
Par: 69
Access: Visitors usually allowed weekdays
Advance contact: Recommended
Documents: Handicap certificate or letter of introduction required
Green fees: Inexpensive

AYR — BELLEISLE GOLF COURSE
Belleisle Park
Doonfoot Road
Ayr, Ayrshire KA7 4DU
Tel: (01292) 441258
Fax: (01292) 442632
Location: 1 mile south of Ayr on main coastal road (A719)
Course length: 6,477 yards (white yards)
Par: 71
Access: Visitors welcome most times
Advance contact: Required
Documents: Handicap certificate or letter of introduction recommended
Green fees: On application

TURNBERRY — TURNBERRY HOTEL GOLF CLUB: AILSA COURSE
Turnberry Hotel
Turnberry, Ayrshire KA26 9LT
Tel: (01655) 31000
Fax: (01655) 31706
Location: Between Girvan and Maybole, on A77
Course length: 6,976 yards (blue yards)
Par: 70
Access: Visitors welcome most times
Advance contact: Recommended
Documents: Handicap certificate or letter of introduction required
Green fees: Expensive

FIFE

ELIE — THE GOLF HOUSE CLUB
Elie, Fife KY9 1AS
Tel: (01333) 330301
Fax: (01333) 330895
Location: 13 miles southeast of St. Andrews
Course length: 6,235 yards (medal yards)
Par: 70
Access: Visitors welcome most days after 10 A.M.

Advance contact: Recommended; play is by ballot on preceding day
Documents: Handicap certificate or letter of introduction required
Green fees: Moderate

CRAIL — CRAIL GOLFING SOCIETY
BALCOMIE GOLF COURSE
Balcomie Clubhouse
Fifeness
Crail, Fife KY10 3XN
Tel: (01333) 450686
Fax: (01333) 450416
Location: 11 miles southeast of St. Andrews
Course length: 5,720 yards (medal yards)
Par: 69
Access: Visitors welcome most times
Advance contact: Recommended
Documents: Handicap certificate or letter of introduction required
Green fees: Inexpensive

ST. ANDREWS — THE OLD COURSE
St. Andrews Links Management Committee
St. Andrews, Fife KY16 9SF
Tel: (01334) 475757
Fax: (01334) 477036
Location: On west side of St. Andrews, on A91
Course length: 6,566 yards (medal yards)
Par: 72
Access: Visitors usually allowed weekdays
Advance contact: Required; tee times determined by ballot
Documents: Handicap certificate or letter of introduction required
Green fees: Expensive

NORTHEAST

DUNDEE — MONIFIETH GOLF LINKS
MEDAL GOLF COURSE
Princes Street
Monifieth, Angus DD5 4AW
Tel: (01382) 532767
Location: 6 miles northeast of Dundee
Course length: 6,651 yards (medal yards)
Par: 71
Access: Visitors usually allowed weekdays
Advance contact: Required
Documents: Handicap certificate or letter of introduction required
Green fees: Moderate

BARRY — PANMURE GOLF CLUB
Panmure Golf Club
Burnside Road
Barry, Angus DD7 7RT
Tel: (01241) 853120
Fax: (01242) 859737
Location: Off A930, 10 miles east of Dundee; 2 miles southwest of Carnoustie
Course length: 6,317 yards (white yards)
Par: 70
Access: Visitors usually allowed weekdays
Advance contact: Required
Documents: Handicap certificate or letter of introduction required
Green fees: Moderate

CARNOUSTIE — CARNOUSTIE GOLF LINKS:
CHAMPIONSHIP GOLF COURSE
Links Management Committee
Links Parade

Carnoustie, Angus DD7 7JE
Tel: (01241) 853789
Fax: (01242) 852720
Location: 12 miles northeast of Dundee by A92
    or A930
Course length: 6,936 yards (medal yards)
Par: 72
Access: Visitors welcome most times
Advance contact: Required
Documents: Handicap certificate or letter of
    introduction required
Green fees: Expensive

MONTROSE — MONTROSE LINKS TRUST: MEDAL COURSE
Traill Drive
Montrose, Angus DD10 8SW
Tel: (01674) 672932
Location: Off A92 Dundee–Aberdeen road;
    1 mile from town center
Course length: 6,443 yards (men's yards)
Par: 71
Access: Visitors welcome most times
Advance contact: Required
Documents: Handicap certificate required
Green fees: Moderate

HIGHLANDS

CRUDEN BAY — CRUDEN BAY GOLF CLUB
Aulton Road
Cruden Bay, Aberdeenshire AB42 7NN
Tel: (01779) 812285
Fax: (01779) 812945
Location: 23 miles north of Aberdeen, off A92
Course length: 6,370 yards (summer yards)

Par: 70
Access: Visitors welcome most times
Advance contact: Recommended
Documents: Letter of introduction required;
    handicap certificate required on weekends
Green fees: Moderate

NAIRN — NAIRN GOLF CLUB
Seabank Road
Nairn, Inverness-shire IV12 4HB
Tel: (01667) 453208
Fax: (01667) 456328
Location: 15 miles northeast of Inverness;
    Seabank Road
Course length: 6,452 yards (white yards)
Par: 71
Access: Visitors welcome most times
Advance contact: Recommended
Documents: Handicap certificate or letter of
    introduction required
Green fees: Moderate

DORNOCH — ROYAL DORNOCH GOLF CLUB: CHAMPIONSHIP GOLF COURSE
Golf Road
Dornoch, Sutherland IV25 3LW
Tel: (01862) 810219
Fax: (01862) 810792
Location: 45 miles north of Inverness; off A9,
    east of town center
Course length: 6,581 yards (white yards)
Par: 70
Access: Visitors welcome most times
Advance contact: Recommended
Documents: Handicap certificate required
Green fees: On application

Index